A PARENT'S GUIDE TO THE BEST

KIDS' COMICS

Choosing Titles Your Children Will Love

Scott Robins & Snow Wildsmith

Published by

Krause Publications, a division of F+W Media, Inc.
700 East State Street • Iola, WI 54990-0001
715-445-2214 • 888-457-2873
www.krausebooks.com

To order books or other products call toll-free 1-800-258-0929
or visit us online at www.krausebooks.com

ISBN-13: 978-1-4402-2994-7
ISBN-10: 1-4402-2994-5

Designed by Sharon Bartsch
Edited by Brent Frankenhoff and Maggie Thompson

Printed in CHINA

On the cover: *Elephant & Piggie* © 2007 & 2010 by Mo Willems; *Yotsuba&!* © Kiyohiko Azuma/ YOTUBA SUTAZIO; *Amelia Rules!* (book and character) © 2011 Jimmy Gownley; *Benny and Penny* © 2009 & 2010 Junior, LLC; *Babymouse* © 2008 by Random House Children's Books. Used by permission of Random House Children's Books, a division of Random House, Inc. *Hikaru No Go* © 1998 by Yumi Hotta, Takeshi Obata/Shueisha, Inc. *Owly* © 2011 Andy Runton; *Smurfs: The Smurf King* © 2010 Peyo Licensed through Lafig Belgium, English translation © 2010 Papercutz; *Bone* © 2011 Jeff Smith; *Mouse Guard* © 2011 David Petersen; figure from *Knights of the Lunch Table* © 2011 Frank Cammuso. In all cases, covers and images were used with permission from the respective copyright holders.

On the back cover: *Gabby & Gator* © 2010 by James Burks; *Zoe and Robot* © 2011 Ryan Sias; *Kapow!* © 2004 George O'Connor; *The Desperate Dog Writes Again* © 2011 Houghton Mifflin Harcourt Children's Books. All rights reserved. In all cases, covers and images were used with permission from the respective copyright holders.

CHAPTER 1:
PRE-K-1
PAGE 12

CHAPTER 2:
2-3
PAGE 45

CHAPTER 3:
4-5
PAGE 86

CHAPTER 4:
6-8
PAGE 146

Jeff Smith and his wife, *Vijaya Iyer*, operate Cartoon Books and its website, *www.boneville.com*, where readers will learn more about their variety of projects, including the award-winning *Bone*.

BY JEFF SMITH AND VIJAYA IYER

Comics and graphic novels are just a part of reading in a different medium, like reading a picture book or a text story or anything like that. A comic book is still just a book.

Comic books provide a wonderful form of reading that is perfect for kids — though, of course, comics aren't *just* for kids. They're a different *kind* of reading, separate from prose — but not *less* than prose. And they work for kids really well, because it requires an extra amount of imagination to take in the pictures: It's a great way for kids to read. You turn the pages; you read left to right, top to bottom — just like any other picture book or prose book.

We both grew up on comics. Vijaya cut her teeth on *Peanuts*, basically learning how to read with those compilations of comic strips. She wasn't a big *comic-book* reader, but comics definitely composed part of her learning how to read — with the help of the pictures.

Like Vijaya, Jeff learned to read through *Peanuts* — by looking at what Snoopy was doing on the top of his doghouse or what kind of lines were making up Charlie Brown's mouth to show that his stomach hurt. And about the time he was 9, he got into the *Pogo* newspaper strip by Walt Kelly, which he still reads today and which works on

A PARENT'S GUIDE TO THE BEST **KIDS' COMICS**

many levels. The strip works on the funny-animal, slapstick level, which he enjoyed as a kid with Kelly's drawings, but it also works on an adult level — with topics covering everything from politics to the newspaper and workaday life. (Jeff didn't see the *Pogo* comic books until much, much later.)

Albert the alligator once said in the Pogo comic-book stories that he "read pictures good." You really *do* have to *read* a picture; even a panel in a comic book that doesn't have any word balloons in it still has to be read by the reader. The kid *still* has to see that picture, process the action or the emotion of the facial expressions, and overlay a passage of time on top of that. As the reader's eye goes over a course of a series of panels, each panel has *information*, whether worded or not: the passage of time, the movement of expression. It's a powerful, but a distinct, form of reading.

We don't think that process changes as the reader grows older. Jeff is still basically a 9-year-old in a 52-year-old body, and he's reading comics in *exactly* the same way as he was reading them decades ago. He can *still* go back and read *Peanuts* and he might have more life experience to bring to the party — but *Peanuts* creator Charles Schulz knew what he was doing. He knew how to write a comic, and the reading experience is identical for child and adult alike.

Yet the experience of understanding is growing, as the reader brings different experiences and methodology to the process. You read things on a different level and differently, as you age. Of course, that's true for prose books, too. When you read *The Lord of the Rings* or *The Odyssey* when you're a teenager, and then you read them again when you're in college or in middle age, you will also bring different life experiences and baggage and get different outcomes. There's no difference *that* way between prose and comics — no difference from the way you process books as a child and then as an adult.

A Parent's Guide to the Best Kids' Comics makes an excellent way to begin to explore children's comics, thanks to the descriptions, the selections, and the parental cautions. And, once you've begun to explore the field, the next step is to let your children go to the library and explore whatever areas they gravitate to. It's very helpful to have guidelines, but really it's ultimately up to the child to pick what interests him or her.

Finally, we need to note that, when we were kids, the ones who read comics were the smart ones. *They* were the eggheads.

Ironically, one of the questions we're most asked about involves the fact that comics seem to work for reluctant readers. We're fine with that. We're glad and we suppose we understand it, because there's fun, the characters have humor, and there's a lot of appeal to the form and the drawings. But we both resist the idea that comics are some kind of a gateway, a "dumbed-down book" for reluctant readers.

Comics are such a *good* way to read that *even* reluctant readers like them!

January 4, 2012
Columbus, Ohio

SCOTT AND SNOW WOULD LIKE TO THANK all of the wonderful writers, artists, publishers, and librarians who create, release, and support children's comics. It is thanks to them that there are so many fantastic graphic novels for children to enjoy. We greatly appreciate all of the publishers who helped us get copies of books, gave us permission to use images, and offered us information, often at the very last moment. Thank you to Maggie and Brent for giving us such a great idea for a book and for working with us to bring it to life. Thank you especially to librarians Robin Brenner, Martha Cornog, Emily Leachman, Eva Volin, and Carlisle Webber, as well as Andrew Woodrow-Butcher from Little Island Comics and Leyla Aker from Viz Media, for their suggestions, encouragement, friendship, and support during this process. All our love to our partners Michael Lamore and Barry Gray for their moral support and patience. Scott and Snow would also like to each thank each other. Writing a book is challenging, but writing one with a dear friend is a challenge to savor.

Additionally, the authors and editors would like to thank the following for their help with this project:

Jason Wells, Abrams Books

Mary Ann Zissimos, Abrams Books

Jay Hosler, Active Synapse

Mel Caylo, Archaia Entertainment

Rik Offenberger, Archie Comics

Alex Segura, Archie Comics

Bessie McNamara, Blue Apple Books

Rob Shaefer, Blue Apple Books

Alexis E. Fajardo, Bowler Hat Comics

Jenny Choy, Candlewick Press

David Hyde, DC

Bridget E. Palmer, Disney

Gina Gagliano, First Second Books

Mimi Ross, Henry Holt

Jennifer Holm, creator

Kate Greene, Houghton Mifflin Harcourt

Marjorie Naughton, Houghton Mifflin Harcourt

Sarah Delaine, Image

Jamie Parreno, Image

Eva Svec, Kids Can Press

A PARENT'S GUIDE TO THE BEST **KIDS' COMICS**

Elizabeth Dingmann, Lerner Books

Victoria Stapleton, Little, Brown

Andrew Woodrow-Butcher, Little Island Comics

Chad Solomon, Little Spirit Bear Productions

Arune Singh, Marvel

James Viscardi, Marvel

Cécile Camberlin, Moulinsart

Cory Casoni, Oni Press

Dayle Sutherland, Orca Books

Michael Petranek, Papercutz

Katie Fee, Penguin

Sara Sheiner, Penguin

Mary Sullivan, Penguin

Kelly Coyle-Crivelli, Random House

Sherri Feldman, Random House

Kate Gartner, Random House

Cathy Goldsmith, Random House

Isabel Warren-Lynch, Random House

Sheila Marie Everett, Scholastic

Orlando Mayumbo, Scholastic

Marilyn Small, Scholastic

Tracy van Stratten, Scholastic

Denise Anderson, Scholastic Canada

Catherine Knowles, Scholastic Canada

Nikole Kritikos, Scholastic Canada

Paul Crichton, Simon & Schuster

Agnes Fisher, Simon & Schuster

Edith Golub, Simon & Schuster

Leigh Stein, Toon Books

Chris Staros, Top Shelf Comix

Leigh Walton, Top Shelf Comix

Jill Thompson, creator

Stacy King, Udon Entertainment

Ed Chavez, Vertical

Leyla Aker, Viz

Jane Lui, Viz

Abby Blackman, Yen Press

Anyone else at these companies we may have missed who assisted with permissions or image procurement.

A special thanks to Whitney Grace for scanning assistance.

Scott Robins is a librarian at the Toronto Public Library and contributor to Salem Press' *Critical Survey of Graphic Novels: Heroes & Superheroes*. He is a contributing blogger for *Good Comics for Kids* via *School Library Journal.com* and is the children's programming director for the annual Toronto Comic Arts Festival. He has also served on the graphic novel selection committee for the Canadian Children's Book Centre's Best Books for Kids and Teens in 2010 and 2011 and was a jury member of the 2011 Joe Shuster Awards in the "Comics for Kids" category.

Snow Wildsmith is a former librarian now working as a writer and book reviewer. She has served on committees for the American Library Association and Young Adult Library Services Association. She reviews graphic novels for *Booklist, ICv2.com, School Library Journal*'s comic-book-review blog *Good Comics for Kids, Unshelved's Book Club*, and Robin Brenner's *No Flying No Tights* review website. She also writes booktalks and creates recommended reading lists for Ebsco's *NoveList* database. McFarland will publish her first books for teens, a nonfiction series on joining the military, in 2012.

INTRODUCTION

KIDS LOVE READING COMICS. We know this because they've told us — by checking out graphic novels from our libraries, by asking us what they should read next, and by telling us that they loved the books we suggested to them.

We've spent much of our careers working to convince our colleagues that kids love comics. Scott pitched the potential of graphic novels to traditional publishers and encouraged comic-book publishers to create material specifically for younger readers. Snow became an advocate for graphic novels in libraries, encouraging librarians to include in their collections graphic novels for all ages.

Our crusade may seem silly, considering that comic books were a staple of kids' recreational reading for a good portion of the 20th century. But somewhere along the line, in the comics industry's struggle to have the medium taken seriously as a way to tell mature, sophisticated stories for adults, comics forgot about kids.

Luckily, creators, librarians, educators, and publishers have worked for several years to increase the number and quality of comics and graphic novels *specifically for kids.* Now, comics are again viewed as tools to encourage a lifelong love of reading — and kids demand them in droves.

Why do kids love comics so much? There's something fundamentally appealing about the combination of text and pictures to tell a story. Comics cross all boundaries — of culture, age, gender, and literacy level — and appeal to both reluctant and voracious readers, to readers new to the English language and to those new to reading in general.

Our goal for this guide is to help you find the graphic novels your kids will love and to keep them reading.

To do that, we selected books that emphasize the wide range of comics written for children. We aimed to select current books, though we did include a few important classics. We attempted to choose titles that are readily available and still in print. Popularity with kids was a factor, but we also tried to highlight hidden gems or future hits. We selected the widest range of genres, content, and reading levels, along with books that will appeal to both boys and girls. We chose books with characters from diverse backgrounds and by creators from all around the world, including North America, Belgium, France, Japan, Germany, the United Kingdom, Australia, and Korea.

You'll note that our list does not include those magazine-like comic books that you may have read growing up. Such comics still exist — but many, if not most, are aimed at older readers. We encourage you to visit your local comic-book shops to see what is being released in periodical form. Don't hesitate to ask store staffers what titles they find to be most appropriate for children.

Since comic books can be difficult for the average reader to find, we focused our attention on graphic novels: book-length stories in both hardcover and paperback form. The word "graphic" simply means "with pictures" and does not refer to graphic or mature content — which is to say, "upsettingly vivid story elements." "Graphic novel" has come to mean any bound book that uses images in sequence, often with text, to tell a story. Graphic novels are easy to find in libraries and bookstores.

You may hear your children talking about manga, the Japanese word for comics. Manga are another type of graphic novel, translated and published in North America but usually read right-to-left, as is the Japanese language, rather than left-to-right, as found in written English. While this printing format can sometimes confuse adult readers, children tend to adapt to reading such volumes with little difficulty.

Snow Wildsmith
Scott Robins

A Parent's Guide to the Best Kids' Comics is designed to provide parents with enough information about each title or series to make informed choices about graphic novels for their children. Each entry provides the following information:

PUBLICATION INFORMATION:

For every title or series, you'll find the names of the creators, some of the volume titles (in the case of a series), the publisher, and the year published. In the appendix that begins on **Page 208,** you'll find a full listing (including all the volumes in the series), including the ISBN (or International Standard Book Number). The ISBN can be used by a library or bookstore to help you find the exact volume you need.

GRADE LEVEL:

The entries are divided into rough grade levels: PreK-1, 2-3, 4-5, and 6-8. These grade levels

Pre-K-1	2-3	4-5	6-8

are general guides and should not discourage readers from reading "up" or reading "down," depending on their own personal reading levels, comfort levels, and/or interests. Sometimes, readers want something fun and easy to read; sometimes they want something more challenging.

GENRES:

Each book or series has been classified according to genre, sometimes multiple genres. These will give you a general idea of what the book is about and can help you choose titles that might appeal to your children, based on their interests. Genres included are:

Adventure: thrilling tales of excitement

Early learning: books that focus on basic educational concepts

Fantasy: tales of magic and other worlds

Historical fiction: books that provide a great way to experience the past

Horror & paranormal: comics that feature ghosts and monsters, both scary and silly

Humor: stories that leave kids laughing

Memoir: tales from a creator's life

Mystery: plots that involve detectives, clues, and something to solve

Non-fiction: true tales of science, history, and more

Romance: stories that celebrate young love

School & family: stories that focus on life at school and in families

Science fiction: tales in which space is only the beginning

Sports & games: exciting stories where characters play to win

Super-hero: adventures of familiar heroes as well as new favorites

Wordless: graphic novels told without words, using only pictures in sequence to tell a story

SUMMARY AND REVIEW:

A brief synopsis summarizes the title or series, and a review details each entry's strengths and appeal.

AWARDS & EDUCATIONAL TIE-INS:

Many of the titles we selected have won awards or been featured on recommended reading lists. Educational tie-ins will allow you — or your child's teacher — to link books to a school curriculum and identify some of the general themes or topics explored in each book. If there are educational materials available online, online links are provided.

HEADS UP:

This section provides alerts to challenging content and will help you decide whether a specific title is appropriate for a specific child. All the books we feature are for children and do not go beyond what's appropriate for each grade level, but these alerts will provide as much information as possible to help make informed choices.

WHAT'S NEXT:

Recommendations for books with similar themes, stories, creators, or structure provide an easy suggestion for your child's next great reading choice.

This is truly a new age of comics for kids. There are many great titles today in addition to those that we've covered here. We urge you to go out to browse. Explore the world of graphic novels for your kids in libraries, bookstores, comic-book shops, and comic-book conventions. Your kids will thank you for it!

Benny and Penny series

Story and art by Geoffrey Hayes

Toon Books, 2008-2011
Color, 32 pages each

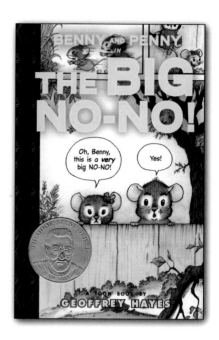

Benny wants to play pirate, but not with Penny, his silly sister. However, when she disappears, it's up to Benny to find her. Then, the two make friends with a new neighbor and have to save their toys from being destroyed by their cousin.

Even though Benny and his sister Penny look like mice, their issues will be familiar to young readers. While they have fun, the two learn important lessons about playing together, behaving, being nice to others, and using their imagination and readers will enjoy themselves as well. Hayes' soft pencil work gives a gentle feeling to his stories, but he carefully avoids babyishness or cutesiness. The simple text works with the images to help early readers navigate through the stories on their own.

IN THIS SERIES:

Benny and Penny in Just Pretend
Benny and Penny in The Big No-No!
Benny and Penny in The Toy Breaker

AWARDS:

2010 Association for Library Service to Children Theodore Seuss Geisel Award Winner (*The Big No-No!*); 2010 Association for Library Service to Children Notable Children's Book (*The Big No-No!*)

EDUCATIONAL TIE-INS:

Sibling relationships; Imagination; Conflict resolution; Lesson plans available at *http://toon-books.com/lp_bpjp.php* (*Just Pretend*), *http://toon-books.com/lp_bpno.*

php (*The Big No-No!*), and *http://toon-books. com/lp_bpt.php* (*The Toy Breaker*); Read online in English, French, Spanish, Russian, and Chinese: *http://toon-books.com/rdr_two. php#bpjp* (*Just Pretend*) and *http://toon-books. com/rdr_two.php#bpno* (*The Big No-No!*)

HEADS UP:

Contains a few minor instances of name-calling.

"WHAT'S NEXT ..."

A COUPLE OF BOYS HAVE THE BEST WEEK EVER

Story and art by Marla Frazee

Harcourt, 2008
Color, 40 pages

Frazee's Caldecott Honor picture book uses graphic-novel elements to tell the story of two friends who have a great time visiting grandparents at the beach. Her art is also drawn in pencil, giving it a similar feel to Hayes' work, and her story has the same gentle humor.

Captain Raptor series

Story by Kevin O'Malley
Art by Patrick O'Brien

Walker, 2005; 2007
Color, 32 pages each

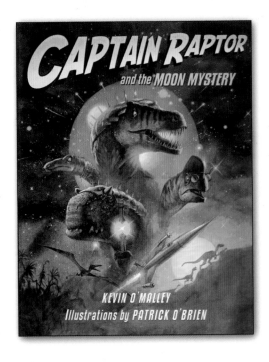

Captain Raptor and the fearless crew of the *USD Megatooth* are the pride of the planet Jurassica. Together with his loyal crew — including Navigator Three Toe, Professor Angleopterous, and Master Sergeant Brickthorous — the Captain investigates mysterious events on faraway moons and keeps space safe from pirates.

A simple story of dinosaurs crewing a spaceship comes to life through O'Brien's hyper-realistic art. The dinosaurs look as if they could have stepped from the pages of an encyclopedia — except for when they wear glasses, use robotic arms, or carry rayguns. The gripping text is reminiscent of old-style comics and forces readers to turn pages to discover the dramatic conclusion to each adventure. Boys who love dinosaurs will eat this series up, and science-fiction-loving parents will enjoy each re-read just as much.

IN THIS SERIES:

Captain Raptor and the Moon Mystery
Captain Raptor and the Space Pirates

AWARDS:

2007 School Library Journal Best Books of the Year List (*Captain Raptor and the Space Pirates*); 2007 Golden Duck Award for Picture Book (*Captain Raptor and the Space Pirates*)

EDUCATIONAL TIE-INS:

Dinosaurs

HEADS UP:

Contains very minor instances of cartoon violence.

"WHAT'S NEXT ..."

ONCE UPON A COOL MOTORCYCLE DUDE
Story by Kevin O'Malley; art by Kevin O'Malley, Carol Heyer, and Scott Goto

Walker Books for Young Readers, 2005
Color, 32 pages

ONCE UPON A ROYAL SUPER BABY
Story by Kevin O'Malley; art by Kevin O'Malley, Carol Heyer, and Scott Goto

Walker Books for Young Readers, 2010
Color, 32 pages

Captain Raptor fans who want another genre mash-up should try these two graphic-novel-inspired picture books, in which a boy and a girl each tells his or her own version of the story with hilarious results.

THE STARSHIP *MEGATOOTH* IS PREPARED FOR BATTLE.

CAPTAIN RAPTOR ASSEMBLES HIS FEARLESS CREW:

PROFESSOR ANGLEOPTEROUS: MASTER ENGINEER.

SERGEANT BRICKTHOROUS: WEAPONS SPECIALIST.

LIEUTENANT THREETOE: ACE PILOT.

"OKAY CREW, *BUCKLE UP,*" SAYS CAPTAIN RAPTOR. "LET'S TEACH THOSE HOOLIGANS A LESSON THEY WON'T FORGET! *3...2...1...*"

Desperate Dog series

Story and art by Eileen Christelow

Clarion Books, 2005; 2010
Color, 32 pages each

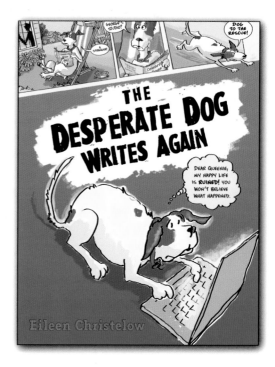

Emma's got a big problem. Her owner, George, only says one thing to her: "Bad dog!" When Emma turns to doggie advice columnist Queenie for help, her advice only gets Emma in more trouble. Now, Emma must figure out how to get George to appreciate her and, later, how to handle a new human in George's life, all on her own. Well … with a little help from the cat.

With pets or not, kids will identify with Emma's feeling of never being able to do the right thing. Her attempts to fix her problems are always funny and consistent with how dogs really act. Kids will laugh at how the animals can talk to each other and how humans never understand them. The brightly colored, cartoonish illustrations move from a mix of picture-book style and graphic-novel art in book one to full comic-book art in book two, showing how comics have become more accepted in children's literature over the past five years.

IN THIS SERIES:
Letters from a Desperate Dog
The Desperate Dog Writes Again

EDUCATIONAL TIE-INS:
Letter writing; Pets; Teaching guide available at *http://www.christelow.com/ classroom/desperatedog.html*

HEADS UP:
Contains two instances of name-calling.

"WHAT'S NEXT …"

DOGGIE DREAMS
Story and art by Mike Herrod

Blue Apple Books, 2011
Color, 40 pages

This early reader from the Balloon Toons line will appeal to readers who wonder what their dog dreams about. The answer will make them laugh!

HUMOR

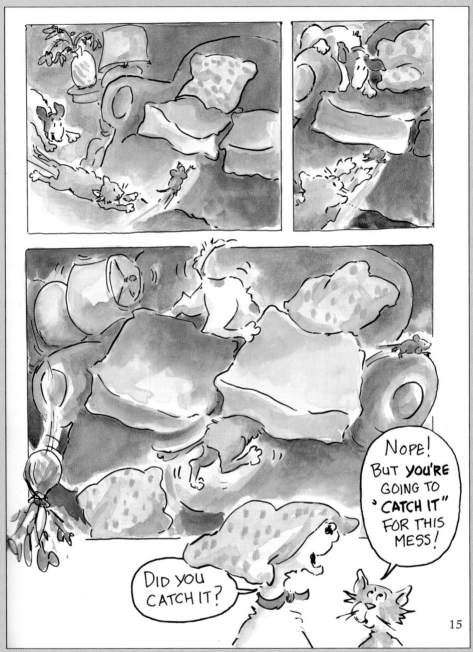

FANTASY • HUMOR • MYSTERY

Detective Blue

Story by Steve Metzger
Art by Tedd Arnold

Scholastic/Orchard Books, 2011
Color, 32 pages

Little Boy Blue, now all grown up, has taken on a job as a detective and solves mysteries in the world of nursery rhymes. When Jack Sprat exclaims that Miss Muffet is missing, Detective Blue takes the case. He searches for clues — examining her tuffet and tasting her curds and whey. After interviewing Little Bo Peep, Humpty Dumpty, and Little Jack Horner, Blue is led to a free concert at Old King Cole's castle, where he meets a spider who gives him the final clue to lead him to the missing Miss Muffet.

Metzger has created a fractured fairytale book for the younger age group — readers will revel in identifying references to their favorite Mother Goose rhymes. Arnold's art newly interprets classic nursery-rhyme characters and captures their silliness in large, bold, colorful panels. In addition to being introduced to the themes of detective stories, children will also enjoy the off-the-wall humor in the main story — and in the backgrounds of each page.

EDUCATIONAL TIE-INS:

Nursery rhymes; Detectives

"WHAT'S NEXT ..."

THE THREE PIGS
Story and art by David Wiesner

Clarion Books, 2001
Color, 40 pages

This fractured interpretation of the traditional Three Little Pigs fairytale offers a more complex adaptation in which the pigs escape their own story and travel through others to outsmart the wolf. Wiesner's award-winning picture book plays with such graphic novel elements as panel borders and word balloons, but young readers will enjoy following this familiar (yet surprisingly fresh) take on the traditional tale.

HECTOR PROTECTOR AND AS I WENT OVER THE WATER: TWO NURSERY RHYMES WITH PICTURES
Story and art by Maurice Sendak

HarperCollins, 2011
Color, 64 pages

Readers with a newfound love of nursery rhymes after identifying the many rhymes in *Detective Blue* might want to discover two lesser-known rhymes as interpreted and illustrated by Maurice Sendak. Using panels and word balloons, Sendak infuses a comic-book sensibility — as well as his signature zany sense of humor — in these two rhymes.

HUMOR

Elephant & Piggie series

Story and art by Mo Willems

Hyperion Books, 2007-2011
Color, 64 pages each

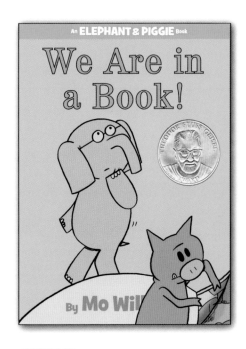

An elephant named Gerald and a pig named Piggie may be best friends but they are also very different. Gerald is a worrier and more emotional, while Piggie is more daring and carefree. The two of them (with occasional animal friends) solve everyday problems, challenges, and dilemmas, often thinking about the other person first. As best friends, they complement each other in every way.

In this series, Willems creates a model for friendship, exploring such traits as sharing, perseverance, inclusivity, helping others, and reassurance. The appeal of these characters and their genuine emotions will get kids on board instantly. Using each page as a single panel, Willems uses varying shapes and styles of word balloons and depicts strong body language of the two characters to tell accessible stories for struggling readers — stories that are also hilarious and will appeal to all. The use of repetition and questioning in the dialogue reinforces literacy skills and will help readers engage with the stories on their own.

IN THIS SERIES:

A full list of titles appears on page 209.

AWARDS:

2009 Association for Library Service to Children Theodore Seuss Geisel Medal (*Are You Ready to Play Outside?*); 2008 Association for Library Service to Children Theodore Seuss Geisel Medal (*There Is a Bird on Your Head*)

EDUCATIONAL TIE-INS:

Friendship

"WHAT'S NEXT ..."

HIPPO AND RABBIT **SERIES**
Story and art by Jeff Mack

THREE SHORT TALES
BRAVE LIKE ME

Scholastic/Cartwheel Books, 2011
Color, 32 pages each

Readers who love the strong friendship themes in *Elephant & Piggie* will enjoy this similar, slightly higher-level series (featuring a hippo and a rabbit) with more panels and more words.

© Text and illustration copyright 2007 & 2010 by Mo Willems

Hocus Pocus

Story by Sylvie Desrosiers
Art by Remy Simard

Kids Can Press, 2011
Color, 32 pages

SYLVIE DESROSIERS • RÉMY SIMARD

While a magician and his dog relax after a grocery trip, Hocus Pocus, a rabbit from the magician's hat, sets his sights on a bunch of carrots poking out of a shopping bag. Hocus tries his best to avoid waking the dog, but the two end up chasing each other, battling wits using soothing violin music, bone-shaped balloons, spilled milk, and ketchup. The two put aside their differences for a split second only to get the attention of the magician, who wakes up to a complete mess.

Desrosiers has created a simple, fun graphic novel packed with slapstick humor and reminiscent of both older cartoons (such as those from Warner Brothers) and modern cartoons of today (such as those on Nickelodeon). Simard's bright, colorful art and attractive character design will appeal to both pre-readers and children just beginning to read. Since the graphic novel is wordless except for sound effects, readers will hone skills in inferring and predicting and gain a better understanding of story sequence and structure.

EDUCATIONAL TIE-INS:

Humor; Story structure

HEADS UP:

Contains minor instances of cartoon violence.

"WHAT'S NEXT ..."

OCTOPUS SOUP
Story and art by Mercer Mayer

Marshall Cavendish, 2011
Color, 32 pages

For another fun wordless graphic novel, check out Mayer's tale of a young octopus who leaves home, only to find himself in a strange world of cars, farmers' markets, and kitchens run by crazed chefs. Mayer's art is more detailed than Simard's and will encourage young readers to explore the wacky details on each page.

Material from *Hocus Pocus* is used by permission of Kids Can Press Ltd., Toronto. Text © 2011 by Sylvie Desrosiers Illustrations © 2011 Rémy Simard

FANTASY • HUMOR

Johnny Boo series

Story and art by James Kochalka

Top Shelf, 2008-2012
Color, 40 pages each

Johnny Boo and Squiggle are best friends who love spending time together and helping each other out. The two have fun while making friends with an ice-cream monster, searching for twinkle power, gathering happy apples, scaring a mean boy who wants to catch them, and even being bored. Luckily Johnny Boo's boo power and Squiggle's squiggle power come in handy, when problems need solving.

Even though Kochalka's series for young readers may seem silly, it explores the range of feelings and emotions a child experiences. Both main characters must face their fears, learn to share, have their feelings hurt, and have fun. The friendship between Johnny Boo and Squiggle is realistic for children at this age with its ups and downs and competitive spirit. There are a few minor instances of potty humor — a focus on the ice-cream monster's butt and reference to the mean little boy having to pee — but nothing to interrupt the delightful adventures of these two ghosts.

IN THIS SERIES:

The Best Little Ghost in the World
Twinkle Power
Happy Apples
The Mean Little Boy
Does Something!

EDUCATIONAL TIE-INS:

Emotions; Friendship; Communication; Ghosts; Bullying (*The Mean Little Boy*)

HEADS UP:

Contains a few minor instances of potty humor.

"WHAT'S NEXT ..."

OTTO'S ORANGE DAY
Story by Jay Lynch
Art by Frank Cammuso

Toon Books, 2008
Color, 40 pages

Young readers craving more offbeat silliness similar to Kochalka's series may want to try this story about a cat who meets a genie who gives him one wish. Impulsively, the cat wishes that the entire world be colored in hues of orange.

SUPER-HERO

Kapow!
Ker-splash!
series

Story and art by George O'Connor

Simon & Schuster/Aladdin, 2007; 2010
Color, 48 pages and 40 pages

"This looks like a job for The Incredible American Eagle and The Amazing Bug Lady!" Two friends with super-powered imaginations have adventures together — fighting Rubber Bandit and defeating the dastardly Manphibian (both also known as "little brother"). But those adventures lead to chaos, and American Eagle and Bug Lady must work together to repair the damage they have caused and to take down an evil bully.

The wonder of O'Connor's story lies in how seamlessly he switches back and forth between the real world and the world of imagination. When he shows the real world, his characters look like a little boy and a little girl, and their life fits into one panel per page. When O'Connor draws what they are imagining, they resemble adult super-heroes, and the drama is heightened through the use of a darker color scheme and double-page spreads without panel borders. There are mild lessons in both books about being responsible and doing what is right, but the message never overwhelms the fun.

IN THIS SERIES:

Kapow!
Ker-splash!

EDUCATIONAL TIE-INS:

Sibling relationships; Imagination

HEADS UP:

Contains minor instances of cartoon violence.

"WHAT'S NEXT ..."

BATMAN: THE STORY OF THE DARK KNIGHT
SUPERMAN: THE STORY OF THE MAN OF STEEL
WONDER WOMAN: THE STORY OF THE AMAZON PRINCESS
Story and art by Ralph Cosentino

Viking Juvenile, 2008-2011
Color, 40 pages each

Young readers who want the history of three of the world's greatest super-heroes will love these picture-book graphic novels that have slightly old-fashioned comic art and plenty of heroism.

EARLY LEARNING • HUMOR

Little Mouse Gets Ready

Story and art by Jeff Smith

Toon Books, 2009
Color, 32 pages

When Little Mouse's mom tells him to get ready for a trip to the barn with his brother and sister, he is excited about all the things he can see and do. With his clothing all laid out, he begins dressing, working from the easiest (his underpants), to the most difficult (buttoning up his shirt). When Mama comes to check on her son, she sees something she didn't expect.

This complete departure from Smith's epic fantasy *Bone* (see page 160) is a deceptively simple story that not only identifies the names of pieces of clothing and shows children the sequence of putting them on, but is also a story of child empowerment and independence. Young readers will view themselves as Little Mouse and cheer on his perseverance, even with difficult tasks. The art is charming, with only one or two panels per page, and delivers plenty of visual jokes, culminating in the punchline at the end of the book.

AWARDS:
2010 Association for Library Service to Children Theodore Seuss Geisel Honor

EDUCATIONAL TIE-INS:
Independence; Clothing; Lesson plan available at *http://toon-books.com/lp_lmo.php*; Read online in English, French, Russian, Spanish, and Chinese at *http://toon-books.com/rdr_one.php#lmo*

"WHAT'S NEXT ..."

BILLY TARTLE IN SAY CHEESE!
Story and art by Michael Townsend

Knopf, 2007
Color, 40 pages

Children who have mastered the skill of dressing themselves and are ready to make decisions about their own clothing choices will appreciate Billy's unusual way of standing out on picture day at school. Townsend's comic is sillier than Smith's but (as in Smith's book) also offers a laugh-out-loud unexpected ending.

CAT THE CAT SERIES
Story and art by Mo Willems

CAT THE CAT WHO IS THAT?
WHAT'S YOUR SOUND HOUND THE HOUND?
LET'S SAY HI TO FRIENDS THAT FLY
TIME TO SLEEP SHEEP THE SHEEP

Balzer and Bray, 2010
Color, 32 pages each

Cat the Cat enjoys asking her other animal friends questions such as what type of animal they are, what sounds they make, and whether or not they can fly. Beginning readers who were entertained by the simple story and surprising ending in Smith's *Little Mouse* will find the same uncomplicated silliness in Willems' series for young children.

© 2009 Jeff Smith

Luke on the Loose

Story and art by Harry Bliss

Toon Books, 2009
Color, 32 pages

While his father catches up with a friend in the park, Luke spots a flock of pigeons and takes the opportunity to chase them. Luke continues to pursue the birds through the park and into the city, forcing his father to get help from the police to find him. Causing chaos as he trails the pigeons, Luke interrupts a marriage proposal at a restaurant, crashes into an ice-cream vendor, and climbs a fire escape to reach the top of a water tower. Exhausted, Luke falls asleep, until the firemen arrive and safely return him to his family.

Bliss' simple chase story is packed with slapstick humor, as Luke charges through the streets of Brooklyn and provides an opportunity for parents to explain that Luke's behavior should not be imitated. The simple, clean art features lots of bold colors and tons of visual gags, as well as inside jokes and references that parents will enjoy explaining to their children. Among Bliss' strengths is depicting characters' facial expressions, and this story includes a wide range of emotions including surprise, fear, and joy. Even children who aren't risk-takers will enjoy Luke's free-spirited adventures.

EDUCATIONAL TIE-INS:

Emotions; City life

"WHAT'S NEXT ..."

THE PUDDLEMAN

Story and art by Raymond Briggs

Red Fox, 2004
Color, 32 pages

Children will see a similarity between Luke and Tom, a young boy who takes his grandfather for a walk, only to wander off and find a strange man carrying puddles on his back. Briggs' surreal tale is not as simple as Bliss' story but contains the same wild spirit of independence and self-discovery.

Mr. Badger and Mrs. Fox series

Story by Brigitte Luciani
Art by Eve Tharlet
Translation by Carol Klio Burrell

Lerner/Graphic Universe, 2010–2011
Color, 32 pages each

Mrs. Fox and her daughter Ginger move in with Mr. Badger and his children (Bristle, Grub, and Berry) after hunters find their burrow. As an only child, Ginger finds it is hard to adjust to having two brothers and a baby sister, and the boys feel the same about their bossy new sister. The three older children learn how to live, work, and play together, while adapting to the parenting styles of their new stepparents.

The kids are the main focus of Luciani's story, which is what makes it a strong choice for young readers trying to understand the complexities of blended families. Ginger, Bristle, and Grub's feelings about each other and their new family are realistic, even told from an animal's point of view. Plenty of humor keeps the story light, but the stories are a little text-heavy for new readers; adults may need to read along. Tharlet's soft art is warm and welcoming, but not girly or babyish, making this a good pick for both genders.

IN THIS SERIES:

#1: The Meeting
#2: A Hubbub
#3: What a Team!

EDUCATIONAL TIE-INS:

Blended families; Sibling relationships; Teamwork (#3: What a Team!)

HEADS UP:

Contains minor instances of name-calling.

"WHAT'S NEXT ..."

PATRICK IN A TEDDY BEAR'S PICNIC AND OTHER STORIES

Story and art by Geoffrey Hayes

Toon Books, 2011
Color, 32 pages

Patrick is an only child (not part of the sort of blended family represented by Ginger and her stepbrothers). Nevertheless, young readers who like the antics of the fox and badger siblings will also enjoy Patrick's attempts to evade a bully, avoid naptime, and have fun on a picnic with Mom. Hayes' pencil work softens his humorous stories and portrays the same grasp of childhood amusements as do Luciani and Tharlet.

Owly series

Story and art by Andy Runton

Top Shelf, 2004-2008
Black and white, 120-160 pages

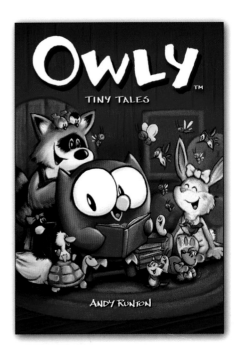

Owly is a kind-hearted, often misunderstood owl who becomes close friends with a worm named Wormy after saving him from drowning during a storm. The two spend their days helping each other with various projects, often with the advice and guidance of Mrs. Raccoon, who owns a plant nursery. In their search to make new friends, Owly and Wormy help other animals in the forest. Such endeavors include rescuing a pair of hummingbirds after they are captured, finding bluebird fledglings lost during a storm, calming a shy flying squirrel, and treating an opossum with an injured paw.

Runton creates iconic, memorable characters that are not only cute but also convey a great deal of emotion. Readers will look to Runton's main characters as a model for their own friendships but will also find stereotypes challenged by Owly's kindness and Wormy's bravery. This series introduces readers to such information as plant care, as well as animal behaviors, eating habits, and habitats. As a wordless graphic novel that uses rebuses, icons, and symbols, *Owly* is accessible at all literacy levels and reinforces inferring skills, a fundamental component in reading comprehension.

IN THIS SERIES:

A full list of titles appears on page 212.

AWARDS:

2006 Eisner Award for Best Publication for a Younger Audience; 2006 Ignatz Award for Best Series; 2005 Ignatz Award for Promising New Talent; 2005 Harvey Award for Best New Talent; 2004 Howard E. Day Memorial Prize

EDUCATIONAL TIE-INS:

Friendship; Nature; Animal habitats; Animal behavior; Teaching guides available at *http://www.andyrunton.com/teaching/*

HEADS UP:

Contains a few strong or frightening scenes.

"WHAT'S NEXT ..."

CHICKEN AND CAT
Story and art by Sara Varon

Scholastic, 2006
Color, 40 pages

CHICKEN AND CAT CLEAN UP
Story and art by Sara Varon

Scholastic, 2009
Color, 48 pages

Readers looking for the kind of sweet, supportive friendship found in *Owly* may want to look at Varon's two wordless graphic novel-inspired picture books. These stories are less complex but use the same kind of appealing characters and expressive art to illustrate strong friendship.

Rick & Rack and the Great Outdoors

Story and art by Ethan Long

Blue Apple Books, 2010
Color, 40 pages

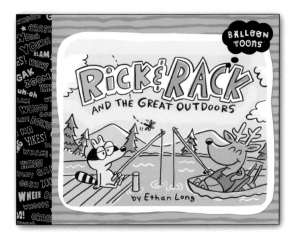

Rack is excited about the great outdoors and is ready for fishing, hiking, tracking, and canoeing. He wants Rick to join him in the fun, but his friend is less convinced of the wonders of the wilderness, worried about the stinky fish, the dangerous canoe, and even the fire-breathing dragon.

This early-reader graphic novel has three separate stories that are tied together by the theme of adventures in the wilderness. Part of the humor comes from the way Long carefully sets up each joke. The punchlines are fitting but won't be overly obvious to new readers. The humor is furthered by his choice to have a deer and a raccoon as his characters. Their human behavior is illustrated in a brightly colored cartoon style, with large, easy-to-follow panels and fonts.

EDUCATIONAL TIE-INS:

Outdoor adventure; Canoeing; Fishing; Hiking; Camping

"WHAT'S NEXT ..."

BENJAMIN BEAR IN FUZZY THINKING
Story and art by Philippe Coudray

Toon Books, 2011
Color, 32 pages

Readers who enjoy humorous stories will want to move on to Coudray's single-page comics that read like *Far Side* cartoons for the elementary school set. Benjamin's antics are silly and offbeat, and the unexpected results of some of his decisions will make both adults and kids laugh. Coudray's art is more realistic than Long's, but his characters are just as much fun.

LUCKY LEAF
Story and art by Kevin O'Malley

Walker, 2005
Color, 32 pages

A young boy and his friends grudgingly venture into the outdoors, but are surprised when they find the final lucky leaf on an autumn-bare tree. O'Malley's story is more realistic than Long's silly tale but both explore the same theme of the reluctant outdoorsman and the unexpected surprises that come with enjoying the outside.

© 2010 Ethan Long

Silly Lilly series

Story and art by Agnes Rosenstiehl

Toon Books, 2008, 2010
Color, 32 pages each

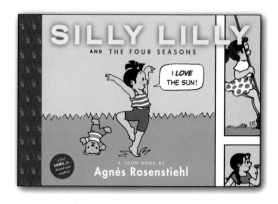

Silly Lilly is a curious little girl who enjoys each day as an opportunity to learn something new along with her stuffed bear, Teddy. First, she explores the seasons and all the great things about them, including picking shells by the beach, eating autumn-ripe apples, and building big snowballs. Next, she tries out new jobs and pretends she is a cook, an acrobat, a teacher, and more for each day of the week.

Rosenstiehl's simple graphic novels are squarely aimed at pre- and early readers and feature minimal text, colorful art, and only two panels per page. With little plot, these books explore concepts including colors, words, and shapes, along with the seasons and the days of the week and are a terrific choice for classroom use for teachers looking to enhance an early-concepts curriculum. Young readers will enjoy the sense of independent exploration, as they accompany Lilly on her discoveries.

IN THIS SERIES:

Silly Lilly and the Four Seasons
Silly Lilly in What Will I Be Today?

EDUCATIONAL TIE-INS:

Seasons; Colors; Opposites (*Silly Lilly and the Four Seasons*); Days of the week; Community jobs (*Silly Lilly in What Will I Be Today?*); Teaching guide available at *http://toon-books.com/ lp_lilly.php*; Read online in English, French, Russian, Spanish, and Chinese at *http://toon-books.com/rdr_one. php#lilly*

"WHAT'S NEXT ..."

YO GABBA GABBA! SERIES
GOOD NIGHT, GABBALAND
Story by J. Torres
Art by Matthew Loux

Oni Press, 2010
Color, 16 pages

GABBA BALL
Story and art by Chris Eliopoulos

Oni Press, 2010
Color, 16 pages

These graphic-novel board books based on the popular Nickelodeon television show are simply written for young readers and feature gentle stories about life in a fun, silly land. Readers who love the bright art and simple fun of *Silly Lilly* will enjoy these collections that offer an excellent way to introduce children to some of the brightest stars currently working in children's comics.

MY NAME IS ELIZABETH
Story by Annika Dunklee
Art by Matt Forsythe

Kids Can Press, 2011
Color, 32 pages

A young girl named Elizabeth adores her name and while attending school, helping her family with chores, and just being a typical little girl, she is quick to remind everyone not to call her by nicknames. Dunklee's story doesn't address any early concepts as in *Silly Lilly*, but both books share a strong, independent protagonist, with plenty of opinions about the world around her.

The Snowman

Story and art by Raymond Briggs

Random House/Dragonfly Books, 1986
Color, 32 pages

RAYMOND BRIGGS

When a boy wakes one morning to see snow falling outside his window, he quickly runs outside to build a snowman. That evening, the boy sees that the snowman has come to life and invites him into his home. The boy shows the snowman the television and his parents' closet and warns him about such dangers as the hot stove. The two share a meal before taking off into the winter sky, flying all over the world until returning home, where the boy says goodbye to his new friend.

Briggs' wordless graphic picture book can be enjoyed by readers of all ages, but his soft, textured pencils make this book ideal for early visual learners. Briggs touches on childhood reference points including bedtime, winter play, dinner time, family, and the home, which will be familiar to young readers. This story of true friendship illustrates that the sharing of experiences can be deep and meaningful. Though the ending of *The Snowman* may be sad, it is an opportunity to discuss the concept of loss with children.

AWARDS:

1979 Boston Globe-Horn Book Award

EDUCATIONAL TIE-INS:

Friendship; Winter; Bedtime

HEADS UP:

Explores the concept of death through metaphor.

"WHAT'S NEXT ..."

THE ADVENTURES OF POLO SERIES
Story and art by Regis Faller
THE ADVENTURES OF POLO
POLO: THE RUNAWAY BOOK
Roaring Brook Press, 2006-2007
Color, 80 pages each

Polo's wordless adventures may not have the same melancholic tone as *The Snowman* but do contain the same spirit of travel, exploration, and friendship. Readers will enjoy the colorful whimsy found in the pages of these two volumes, as Polo travels the world, meets strange new people, and, ultimately, finds happiness at home..

"Book Cover," © 1978 by Random House Children's Books, from *The Snowman* by Raymond Briggs, © 1978 by Raymond Briggs. Used by permission of Random House Children's Books, a division of Random House, Inc. Interior illustration © 1978 by Random House Children's Books, from *The Snowman* by Raymond Briggs, © 1978 by Raymond Briggs. Used by permission of Random House Children's Books, a division of Random House, Inc.

Zoe and Robot: Let's Pretend!

Story and art by Ryan Sias

Blue Apple Books, 2011
Color, 40 pages

Zoe wants to play pretend and go mountain climbing, but Robot just can't get the hang of using his imagination. She tries everything she can think of to get him to see the majestic mountain, feel the breeze, and shiver in the cold, but he just sees a mound of pillows, feels a fan blowing, and isn't cold at all. Zoe must get creative to help him learn how to pretend.

Sias' story is a terrific choice for young readers. The text is simple, especially Robot's basic responses, and the panel images match what is being said, helping new readers figure out the text independently. The cute, cartoon art is eye-catching with the use of bright colors. Zoe's tomboyish nature along with the boy-friendly Robot and the book's light humor makes this a great pick for boys as well as girls.

EDUCATIONAL TIE-INS:

Imagination

"WHAT'S NEXT ..."

CAT SECRETS

Story and art by Jeff Czekaj

Balzer + Bray, 2011
Color, 32 pages

In this interactive graphic-novel picture book, three cats are ready to open the top-secret book of cat secrets, but, first, readers must prove they are cats by meowing, purring, stretching, and more. The large, panel-less pages make this a good choice for storytime where listeners can have fun pretending to be cats while they stretch their imaginations and learn to follow directions.

TRACTION MAN SERIES

Story and art by Mini Grey

TRACTION MAN IS HERE!
TRACTION MAN MEETS TURBO DOG

Knopf, 2005, 2008
Color, 32 pages each

When he receives a new toy called Traction Man for Christmas, a young boy begins a series of action-figure adventures all through his home, in his backyard, and all the way to his grandmother's house. Grey's story is all about how the power of child's imagination can transform everyday objects into creatures, allies, and obstacles and it reinforces Zoe's efforts to get Robot to pretend and have fun.

© 2011 Ryan Sias.

In the Night Kitchen

Story and art by Maurice Sendak

HarperCollins, 1970
Color, 40 pages

FANTASY

A young boy named Mickey wakes in the middle of the night to the sound of loud, strange noises. After shouting for quiet, he unexpectedly tumbles through the floor into the Night Kitchen and meets three identical, jolly-looking bakers. The three bakers are in the middle of making cakes, mistake Mickey for milk, and bake him into the cake. Mickey frees himself from the cake, kneads himself an airplane from bread dough, and helps to collect milk for the bakers' batter.

Best known for the classic picture book *Where the Wild Things Are*, Sendak offers here a surreal yet familiar look into the imagination and dreams of a child. Readers will delight in the details and scale of the art — Mickey is a true explorer in the larger-than-life world of the Night Kitchen. Playful text, dialogue, and sound effects make this book great for reading aloud. Mickey appears nude in parts of the story, making this one of the more controversial books in children's literature.

AWARDS:

1970 New York Times Outstanding Book of the Year; 1971 Caldecott Honor Book; 1970 School Library Journal Best Book; 1970 New York Times Best Illustrated Book; 1970 ALA Notable Children's Book; 1970 Library of Congress Children's Books

EDUCATIONAL TIE-INS:

Dreams; Imagination

HEADS UP:

Contains some nudity.

"WHAT'S NEXT ..."

TUESDAY
Story and art by David Wiesner

Clarion Books, 1991
Color, 32 pages

Readers looking for another strange and surreal story should try this graphic-novel-style picture book about a seemingly ordinary Tuesday night when a group of frogs soar through a small town on floating lily pads.

The Adventures of Daniel Boom, aka Loud Boy series

Story by D.J. Steinberg
Art by Brian Smith

Penguin/Grosset & Dunlap, 2008-2010
Color, 96 pages each

When the child-hating scientists at Kid-Rid Corporation unleash a Behavio-Ray that will make all children quiet and well-behaved, it backfires, giving four children amazing super-powers. Daniel Boom, aka Loud Boy, has no indoor voice. Rex Rodriguez, aka Destructo-Kid, unleashes chaos wherever he goes. Violet Fitz, aka Tantrum Girl, uses rage to get her way. Sid Down, aka Fidget, has the power of Perpetual Motion. Together with Daniel's genius kid sister, Jeannie S. Boom, aka Chatterbox, the heroes must protect kids everywhere from the forces of old people.

Any child who has ever been told to "be quiet" or "sit still" will enjoy Steinberg's silly, kid-power tale. The five main characters know their strengths come from their greatest weaknesses and struggle to control themselves and behave normally. Readers will root for them, as the heroes realize they have the power to save the world. Smith's bright art resembles a Saturday-morning cartoon, and the story contains plenty of action to keep the pages turning and enough humor to get readers giggling.

IN THIS SERIES:

#1: Sound Off!
#2: Mac Attack!
#3: Game On!
#4: Grow Up!

© Text copyright 2008 & 2009 by DJ Steinberg
Pictures copyright 2008 & 2009 by Brian Smith

EDUCATIONAL TIE-INS:

Behavior issues; Friendship

HEADS UP:

Contains some cartoon violence and minor instances of name-calling.

"WHAT'S NEXT ..."

HYPERACTIVE
Story by Scott Christian Sava
Art by Joseph Bergin III

IDW, 2008
Color, 112 pages

Joey Johnson must evade evil scientists, when his hyperactivity speeds up to a super-powered level, reminiscent of Daniel and his friends' hilarious attempts to control their own abilities.

ADVENTURE • HUMOR • SUPER-HERO

Babymouse series

Story by Jennifer L. Holm and Matthew Holm
Art by Matthew Holm

Random House, 2005-2011
Black and white with pink (vol. 9 is black and white with orange), 96 pages each

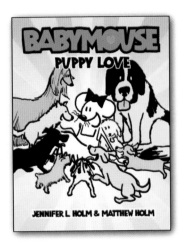

Babymouse is the mouse-next-door, stuck with an annoying little brother, whiskers that frizz, a phobia of fractions, and a burning desire to be as popular as the school's queen bee, Felicia Furrypaws. But whether Babymouse is selling cupcakes to raise money for the library, trying to learn to play the flute, building a derby car, or going to wilderness camp, her overactive imagination — not to mention her love of cupcakes and books — gets her in trouble.

The Holms' series may appear to be about a mouse but, in reality, Babymouse is a stand-in for the very girls who read her stories. Babymouse's problems are familiar, and readers will appreciate the opportunity to laugh at them. Most of the books have messages about the importance of true friendship, being yourself, and determination, but the stories are funny, rather than preachy. Matt Holm's cartoon art brings to life not only Babymouse's real world, but also her fantastic leaps of imagination. The omniscient — and snarky — narrator brings an extra level of humor to the series. The pink covers and abundance of hearts marks this as a sure pick for girls.

IN THIS SERIES:
A full list of titles appears on page 214.

AWARDS:
2006 Association for Library Service to Children Notable Children's Book (#1: *Queen of the World*)

EDUCATIONAL TIE-INS:
Bullying; Cliques and popularity; Friendship; Self-esteem; Body image; Sibling relationships (*Beach Babe*); School life; Sports (*Our Hero*; *Skater Girl*); Pet ownership (*Puppy Love*); Performing arts (*Rock Star*; *The Musical*); Mathematics (*Dragonslayer*); Science (*Mad Scientist*); Holidays (*A Very Babymouse Christmas*)

HEADS UP:
Contains minor instances of cartoon violence and some name-calling.

"WHAT'S NEXT ..."

THE BABY-SITTERS CLUB SERIES
Story by Ann M. Martin
Adaptation and art by Raina Telgemeier

KRISTY'S GREAT IDEA
THE TRUTH ABOUT STACY
MARY ANNE SAVES THE DAY
CLAUDIA AND MEAN JANINE

Scholastic/Graphix, 2005-2008
Black and white, 144-186 pages

Telgemeier's adaptation of Martin's hugely popular tween-age series about four friends who start a babysitting service will appeal to readers who love the realism and humor of *Babymouse*, as well as its focus on building friendship and being true to oneself.

"Book Cover," © 2008 by Random House Children's Books, from *Babymouse #8 Puppy Love* by Jennifer L. Holm and Matthew Holm. Used by permission of Random House Children's Books, a division of Random House, Inc. Interior from *Babymouse: Beach Babe* by Jennifer L. Holm and Matthew Holm, © 2005 by Jennifer L. Holm and Matthew Holm. Used by permission of Random House Children's Books, a division of Random House, Inc.

Binky series

Story and art by Ashley Spires

Kids Can Press, 2009-2011
Color, 64 pages each

As a certified space cat, Binky protects his human family and the secrets of F.U.R.S.T. (Felines of the Universe Ready for Space Travel) from alien invaders who happen to be common bugs. Training hard for his mission, Binky secretly: builds a spaceship out of household items; ventures into outer space to rescue Ted, his stuffed purple mousie; and contends with Gracie, a new perfectly mannered cat who ends up being more than she seems.

Spires explores imagination with tongue-in-cheek humor — Binky believes that he lives in a space station, that bugs are aliens, and that he is a space cat. Readers will find hilarious the ambiguity of whether these things are true. Loaded with sight gags, this series also uses narration, sound effects, and panel and word balloon shapes for multiple levels of wit and includes a few instances of "space gas" and the use of the word "fart" for extra humor. With few words per page, clear layouts, and a character that pops off the page, this series will appeal to most elementary-school students at all reading levels.

IN THIS SERIES:

Binky the Space Cat
Binky to the Rescue
Binky under Pressure

EDUCATIONAL TIE-INS:

Imagination; Cats; Teaching guide available at *http://www. kidscanpress.com/Assets/Books/ w_BinkyTheSpaceCat_2028/PDFs/ BinkyTheSpaceCat_2028_storytime.pdf*

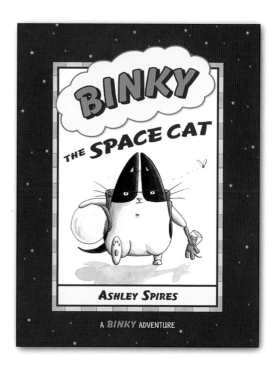

A *BINKY* ADVENTURE

HEADS UP:

Contains a few minor instances of potty humor.

"WHAT'S NEXT ..."

THE ADVENTURES OF PANDA MAN SERIES
Story by Sho Makura
Art by Haruhi Kato

PANDA MAN TO THE RESCUE!
PANDA MAN AND THE TREASURE HUNT
PANDA MAN VS. CHIWANDA

Viz, 2010-2011
Black and white with color, 96 pages each

Panda Man possesses the power of stinky feet and long farts, part of what makes him the "greatest hero in the world." Kids who laugh at Binky's skewed perspective on reality will laugh at these graphic-novel hybrids, which show Panda Man's laziness and gluttony, but also his determination to win.

Dragon Puncher series

Story and art by James Kochalka

Top Shelf, 2010-2011
Color, 40 pages each

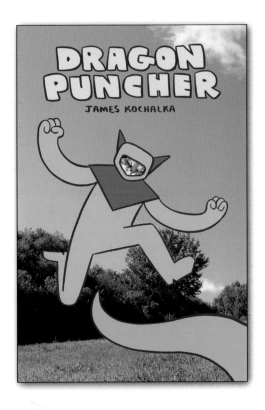

Dragon Puncher, the greatest super-hero of all time, exists only to punch dragons, but the silly Spoon-E keeps getting in his way. When Dragon Puncher breaks Spoon-E's wooden Spoony Spoon, that *should* be the end of it, but the little monster actually helps him defeat a dragon. Together, the hero and his apparent sidekick fight dragons on land and sea, even when the annoying Monster Slapper gets in the way.

Kochalka uses an original concept for his art: Backgrounds and characters' faces are photographs (of Kochalka, his sons, and his cats), but the character bodies and the text balloons are drawn in a simple style, using bold, primary colors. The kid-friendly art, oddball storyline, and just the right amount of gross-out humor — combined with lots of action and wacky original super-heroes — make this ideal for readers who want a good laugh.

IN THIS SERIES:

Book 1: Dragon Puncher
Book 2: Dragon Puncher Island

EDUCATIONAL TIE-INS:

Mixed-media art; Friendship

HEADS UP:

Contains some cartoon violence, some name-calling, and some mild potty humor.

"WHAT'S NEXT ..."

TIGER MOTH SERIES

Story by Aaron Reynolds
Art by Erik Lervold

A full list of titles appears on page 215.

Capstone/Stone Arch, 2007-2008
Color, 40 pages each

Reynolds' and Lervold's series about a ninja in training and his sidekick and their work fighting insect evil will appeal to *Dragon Puncher* fans who like their super-hero stories filled with earnest heroes, lots of action, plenty of puns and silliness, and just a touch of gross-out humor.

Fashion Kitty series

Story and art by
Charise Mericle Harper

Disney/Hyperion, 2005-2011
Color, 96-112 pages

An accident involving a birthday wish, a loose shelf, a stack of books, and a chocolate cake unexpectedly gives Kiki Kittie the ability to turn into Fashion Kitty, the super-hero who handles fashion emergencies. As Fashion Kitty, Kiki helps her friends and classmates solve such sticky issues as developing their own styles, wearing school uniforms, and handling a fashion bully. But keeping her super-powers a secret is hard for Kiki, especially when her best friend thinks that Kiki really hates Fashion Kitty.

Even though the main subject of Harper's series — fashion — may seem unimportant, she uses it to deliver strong messages about respecting oneself, kindness, and developing personal style instead of following the herd. In addition to simple, child-like, three- or four-toned art, each volume has a special full-color insert with such activities as mix-and-match or paper dolls. Fashion Kitty's adventures are gentle enough for young readers, but older girls will also find them appealing.

IN THIS SERIES:

A full list of titles appears on page 216.

EDUCATIONAL TIE-INS:

Self-esteem; Fashion

"WHAT'S NEXT ..."

ZOEY ZETA AND THE SISTERS OF POWER SERIES
Story by Robert Simon
Art by Tomomi Sarafov

#1 FAMILY SECRETS
#2 ARMY OF MEAN

Zeta Comics, 2010-2011
Color, 50-52 pages

Readers looking for a more traditional super-hero tale that still has plenty of girl-power will enjoy this self-published series about three sisters who mysteriously develop super-powers. With his own daughters in mind, Simon wrote this series to fill the gap of engaging science-fiction stories with strong female lead characters.

PRINCESS CANDY SERIES
Story by Michael Dahl
Art by Jeff Crowther

A full list of titles appears on Page 216.

Capstone/Stone Arch, 2010-2011
Color, 40 pages each

Halo Nightly lives every child's dream: She gains super-powers after being given magical candy by her Aunt Pandora. Readers who love *Fashion Kitty*'s fun (slightly girl-focused) take on super-heroes will also enjoy Dahl's action-filled plots and Crowther's bright, eye-catching art.

Gabby & Gator

Story and art by James Burks

Yen Press, 2010
Color, 186 pages

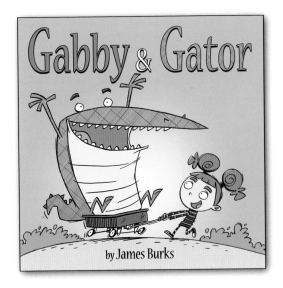

After being flushed down a toilet by a young boy, Gator has made the sewers his home, surfacing occasionally to eat a dog or two to satisfy his uncontrollable hunger. Meanwhile, Gabby, an eco-conscious, shy young girl starts her day with a list of tasks, including finding a friend who will accept her for who she is. Gator encounters Gabby being harassed by a bully and scares him away. The two become unexpected friends and must face their fears together, when Animal Control captures Gator.

Burks delivers a hilarious story packed with off-the-wall wit, visual jokes, and occasional cartoon violence, but no worse than what viewers see in a Nickelodeon cartoon. Great for newly independent readers, this features large, open panels with only a few per page, sparse text, and lots of visual appeal. Burks seamlessly integrates messages including anti-bullying, acceptance of others, and awareness of the environment into the story without being heavy-handed or preachy.

EDUCATIONAL TIE-INS:

Environmental awareness; Bullying; Self-esteem

HEADS UP:

Contains minor instances of cartoon violence.

"WHAT'S NEXT ..."

LUZ SEES THE LIGHT
Story and art by Claudia Davila

Kids Can Press, 2011
Black and white with brown, 96 pages

Readers who enjoy Gabby's passion for the environment might enjoy Luz' equal enthusiasm, as she explores sustainable living with her friends and family. Davila offers kid-friendly environmental tips throughout the story and, at the end of the book, provides readers with skills to make changes in their own world: perfect for classroom lessons on conservation and environmental sustainability.

ADOPT A GLURB
Story and art by Elise Gravel

Blue Apple Books, 2010
Color, 40 pages

Younger readers who love the idea of having a wacky pet, as in *Gabby & Gator*, but who aren't quite ready for the length of Burks' graphic novel, will enjoy *Adopt a Glurb*. Gravel's mock pet care manual tells kids all about how to take care of a glurb, offering plenty of laughs along the way.

Geronimo Stilton series

Story by "Geronimo Stilton"
Concept by Elisabetta Dami
Art by Lorenzo de Pretto (#1 and #2),
Ambrogio M. Piazzoni (#3), Wasabi Studio
(#4), Giuseppe Facciotto (#5), Giuseppe
Ferrario (#7), Federica Salfo (#8) Graphics
by Michaela Battaglin and Marta Lorini
Translation by Nanette McGuinness

NBM/Papercutz, 2009-2012
Color, 56 pages each

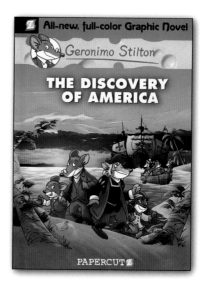

Geronimo Stilton edits *The Rodent's Gazette*, the most important newspaper on Mouse Island. When his best friend, Professor Volt, invents a machine that warns of dangerous changes to the past, Geronimo and his friends and family must use the Speedrat time machine to prevent drastic changes to the present. Geronimo and his friends stop the Pirate Cats from such actions as: scaring Christopher Columbus' crew into mutiny, putting a new face on the Sphinx, renaming the Coliseum, taking credit for Marco Polo's journeys, hunting a woolly mammoth, and stealing the Mona Lisa.

These graphic novels are a spin-off of the popular *Geronimo Stilton* chapter-book series, adding a time-travel component to Geronimo's adventures. Readers will love such verbal and visual humor as puns, wordplay, and slapstick comedy. Each adventure is based on real historical events, and educational notes are added between panels, giving readers the information they need to understand the setting. The art is as bright and cheerful as the art of the series of novels. Even though the text for the graphic novels is printed in a smaller font, which may challenge some readers, the repetitious nature of the series will attract reluctant readers.

IN THIS SERIES:

A full list of titles appears on page 216.

EDUCATIONAL TIE-INS:

Reporters; Christopher Columbus (#1); Ancient Egypt (#2); Ancient Rome (#3); Marco Polo and Kublai Kahn (#4); Ice Age (#5); Leonardo da Vinci and the Mona Lisa (#6); Dinosaurs (#7); Wolfgang Amadeus Mozart (#8); Johannes Gutenberg and the printing press (#9); Reading group guide and puzzles for *#1: The Discovery of America* available at *http://www.papercutz.com/stilton/stiltongames.pdf*

HEADS UP:

Contains minor instances of cartoon violence and some name-calling.

"WHAT'S NEXT ..."

GOOD TIMES TRAVEL AGENCY SERIES
Story by Linda Bailey
Art by Bill Slavin

A full list appears on Page 217.

Kids Can Press, 2000-2004
Color, 48 pages each

When three siblings stumble upon a mysterious travel agency that can transport them back in time, they find themselves thrown in the middle of an assortment of ancient civilizations. While Bailey and Slavin's stories are not as high-stakes adventurous as Geronimo Stilton's exploits, readers with an interest in history and peoples of the past will devour this fact-filled series.

Guinea Pig: Pet Shop Private Eye series

Story by Colleen AF Venable
Art by Stephanie Yue

Lerner/Graphic Universe, 2010-2011
Color, 48 pages each

In Mr. Venezi's pet store, Hamisher, a mystery-obsessed, talkative, high-energy hamster, convinces Sasspants, a bookish guinea pig, to become the shop's resident private investigator. Sasspants reluctantly attempts to solve mysteries by looking for clues and interviewing the various pet store animals, all of whom have their own strange quirks. The detective duo must solve the mystery of Mr. Venezi's missing sandwiches, the disappearance of the store's mice, the crime of defaced pet cage signs, and even the vanishing of Mr. Venezi himself.

This series' friendly picture-book size and colorful art will attract reluctant readers, but the substantial amount of text may challenge new readers. Venable writes a story with loads of laughs in both the witty dialogue and the personalities of her quirky animal characters. In addition to the two lead characters, such supporting characters as the dim-witted fish and the celebrity-obsessed chinchillas are equally hilarious. There are a few instances of name-calling between characters with strong personalities, and Hamisher often uses the phrase "aw poo." The last two pages of each book provide readers with supplemental information regarding the concepts introduced, including animal profiles, jobs working with animals, and the conventions of the mystery genre.

HUMOR • MYSTERY

IN THIS SERIES:

#1: *Hamster and Cheese*
#2: *And Then There Were Gnomes*
#3: *The Ferret's a Foot*
#4: *Fish You Were Here*

EDUCATIONAL TIE-INS:

Detectives; Animal behavior; Pets

HEADS UP:

Contains some instances of name-calling.

"WHAT'S NEXT ..."

ZIG AND WIKKI IN SOMETHING ATE MY HOMEWORK
Story by Nadja Spiegelman
Art by Trade Loeffler

Toon Books, 2010
Color, 40 pages

Readers who enjoyed the combination of humor and fun animal facts throughout all four *Guinea Pig: Pet Shop Private Eye* books may enjoy this silly story about a pair of aliens who come to Earth searching for a pet in order to complete an already late homework assignment.

Kit Feeny series

Story and art by Michael Townsend

Random House, 2009
Black and white with orange, 96 pages each

Kit, a young bear, loves comic books, grand adventures, and his best friend, Arnold. After a failed attempt to bring Arnold along when his parents decide to move, Kit must learn how to make new friends on his own and deal with a bully who thinks he's funny when he's not. Then, Kit has to figure out how to find money to buy his mother the best birthday present or lose a bet to his annoying sisters.

Kit is a bear, but his problems and adventures are the same as those of human boys, with the addition of "stupidly awesome" humor. Expect barfing, silliness involving a Hawaiian shirt, and a crazy birthday present — but also a non-violent way of handling a bully — all of which adds up to a lot of fun for readers. Townsend's deceptively simple art has the same kid appeal as Dav Pilkey's work on *Captain Underpants*. Touching emotions don't detract from the fun and help tie the stories together.

IN THIS SERIES:

On the Move
The Ugly Necklace

AWARDS:

2010 Gryphon Award Honor from the Center for Children's Books at the Graduate School of Library and Information Science at the University of Illinois at Urbana-Champaign

EDUCATIONAL TIE-INS:

Moving; Friendship; Bullying: (*On the Move*); Family (*The Ugly Necklace*)

HEADS UP:

Contains some potty humor and name-calling.

"WHAT'S NEXT ..."

FRANKIE PICKLE SERIES

Story and art by Eric Wight

FRANKIE PICKLE AND THE CLOSET OF DOOM
FRANKIE PICKLE AND THE PINE RUN 3000
FRANKIE PICKLE AND THE MATHEMATICAL MENACE

Simon & Schuster, 2009-2011
Black and white, 96 pages each

Wight's hybrid series — half graphic-novel chapters, half prose chapters — will appeal to readers who enjoy Kit's take on life. Frankie's vivid imagination is let loose, as he tries to clean his room, build a derby car, and survive a math test — all illustrated in a sharp, retro style that is both kid-friendly and hip.

Long Tail Kitty

Art and story by Lark Pien

Blue Apple Books, 2009
Color, 51 pages

Long Tail Kitty is a playful and sociable cat who loves sharing his home and surroundings with everyone. Whether he's spending time with long-term friends — Bernice the dog or a family of visiting aliens — or making new friends — a feisty bee or a mouse who loves to skate — Long Tail Kitty always manages to ensure everyone has fun.

Pien's five short tales about Long Tail Kitty's town and his friends are simple and convey the warmth usually found in picture books for young children. The cute characters, soft watercolor art, and silly dialogue make this a great book for parents to read with their children. Slightly older readers will enjoy the level of wit and the innocent off-color humor, such as when Long Tail Kitty refers to his "bum" or one of the alien children exclaims that he has to go "wee." The title character's interaction with his various friends can be used to start conversations about seeing the good in *all* people and the importance of friendships. The final two pages of the book include instructions on how to draw Long Tail Kitty for aspiring young cartoonists.

EDUCATIONAL TIE-INS:

Friendship; Neighborhoods and communities

HEADS UP:

Contains a few minor instances of potty humor.

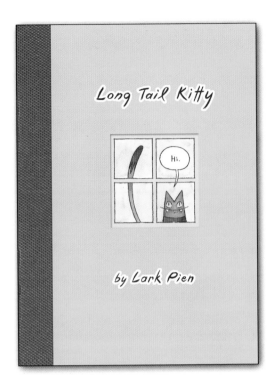

"WHAT'S NEXT ..."

THE SUPER CRAZY CAT DANCE
Story and art by Aron Nels Steinke

Blue Apple Books, 2010
Color, 40 pages

Fans of *Long Tail Kitty*, and cat stories in general, will smile as Steinke's unnamed main character navigates her way through a cartoonish world filled with kitties, spouting poetry as she goes. His art features bright colors on black backgrounds, making this a good choice for bedtime reading. Steinke's book can also be used as a fun way to talk about poetry and art with older children, making it a nice choice for classroom use in language arts and/or art class.

HUMOR

Lunch Lady series

Story and art by Jarrett J. Krosoczka

Knopf, 2009-2011
Black and white with yellow, 96 pages each

Three kids — Hector, Terrance, and Dee — discover that their cafeteria lady has a secret: She not only serves daily meals to students, she also fights crime. With the help of her sidekick, Betty (who creates an array of effective crime-fighting cafeteria-inspired gizmos), Lunch Lady takes down any threat to school or students, including robotic substitute teachers, power-hungry librarians, vengeful authors, camp swamp monsters, insane bus drivers, and thieving museum directors. The three keep Lunch Lady's true identity secret but often join the crime-fighting fun, calling themselves The Breakfast Bunch.

Krosoczka's early-reader series combines over-the-top super-heroics, goofy villains, and dynamic action sequences, all of which add up to fun for both girl and boy readers. Lunch Lady's silly dialogue and Betty's increasingly outrageous gadgets are a great way to introduce puns to young readers. The familiar school setting — along with simple, yet striking art — makes this series an easy entry point. The positive messages — including standing up for oneself, trying new things, and being honest — will win over parents.

IN THIS SERIES:

And the Cyborg Substitute
And the League of Librarians
And the Author Visit Vendetta
And the Summer Camp Shakedown
And the Bake Sale Bandit
And the Field Trip Fiasco

EDUCATIONAL TIE-INS:

Teachers; School; Bullying

HEADS UP:

Contains some cartoon violence.

"WHAT'S NEXT ..."

MAGIC PICKLE
Story and art by Scott Morse

Scholastic/Graphix, 2008
Color, 112 pages

Morse's graphic novel about a molecularly enhanced super-pickle called Weapon Kosher, who must defeat a similarly enhanced group of evil produce, contains the same melodramatic tone, high action, and silly food puns as appear in *Lunch Lady*. Morse's intricate art may require a bit more attention than Krosoczka's but delivers similar fun.

Magic Trixie series

Story and art by Jill Thompson
Lettering by Jason Arthur

HarperTrophy, 2008-2009
Color, 94 pages each

Magic Trixie is a fun, outgoing young witch, but her family always interrupts her grand plans. Her parents tell her she's too young to use their wands and spell books; her grandparents won't get her a dragon; and everyone makes her brush her teeth and take a bath at night. They also tell her that being a good sister means taking care of the baby, but Magic Trixie is tired of being bossed around. She hopes that spending the night at her friends' houses or finding the perfect item for show-and-tell or even turning her sister into a dragon won't make her parents too mad.

Kids will understand Magic Trixie's frustrations (even if they don't have a younger sibling) and her desires to do grown-up things without causing problems. Adults will laugh sympathetically with Magic Trixie's parents, while kids enjoy the chaos she causes. Thompson's watercolor art brings the fantasy setting to vivid life, with many details that refer to traditional horror stories. Even though the characters are witches, werewolves, mummies, monsters, and vampires, the stories are sweet with nothing scarier than a childhood tantrum.

IN THIS SERIES:

Magic Trixie
Magic Trixie Sleeps Over
Magic Trixie and the Dragon

AWARDS:

2009 Will Eisner Comic Industry Award for Best Painter/Multimedia Artist

EDUCATIONAL TIE-INS:

Sibling relationships; Family; Bedtime (*Magic Trixie Sleeps Over*)

HEADS UP:

Contains minor cartoon violence and name-calling.

"WHAT'S NEXT ..."

STICKY BURR SERIES
Story and art by John Lechner

ADVENTURES IN BURRWOOD FOREST
THE PRICKLY PERIL
Candlewick, 2008-2009
Color, 56 pages each

Unlike other burrs who enjoy prickly things, Sticky Burr — who enjoys art and music rather than prickly things — must save the other burrs in Burrwood Forest from a bully named Scurvy Burr. Readers who enjoyed the magical spin on everyday elements in *Magic Trixie* will enjoy Sticky Burr's adventures with friends, family, and school.

Nursery Rhyme Comics: 50 Timeless Rhymes from 50 Celebrated Cartoonists

Art by various

First Second, 2011
Color, 120 pages

Fifty different comic-book, comic-strip, and picture-book artists are allowed free rein to interpret 50 classic nursery rhymes, jump rope songs, and children's poems. The results are a fresh mix of beautiful images, silly twists on the tales, and unusual visions.

When children read this collection of nonsensical rhymes, they will laugh at the sillier entries, and adults will appreciate the ones that are more serious or contemplative. The interpretations range from a somber, but still child-friendly, retelling of *Solomon Grundy* to a beautifully romantic illustration of the poem *The Owl and the Pussycat*. The wide variety of stories is designed to appeal to every kind of reader, with rhymes at which to sigh, smile, or laugh out loud.

EDUCATIONAL TIE-INS:

Nursery rhymes; Poetry; Artistic interpretation

HEADS UP:

Contains some cartoon violence, one minor bit of potty humor, and one minor instance of nudity.

"WHAT'S NEXT ..."

GRAPHIC SPIN SERIES
Story and art by various

SHIVERS, WISHES, AND WOLVES: STONE ARCH FAIRY TALES VOLUME ONE

Contains four *Graphic Spin* titles: *Red Riding Hood*, *Jack & the Beanstalk*, *Cinderella*, and *Rumpelstiltskin*.

SECRETS, MONSTERS, AND MAGIC MIRRORS: STONE ARCH FAIRY TALES VOLUME TWO

Contains five *Graphic Spin* titles: *Beauty and the Beast*, *Rapunzel*, *Princess and the Pea*, *Snow White*, and *Thumbelina*.

Capstone/Stone Arch, 2012
Color, 176 pages each

Capstone's *Graphic Spin* series offers readers different artistic interpretations of classic folktales and fairy tales, making the series a nice companion to *Nursery Rhyme Comics*.

98

Okie Dokie Donuts

Story and art by Chris Eliopoulous

Top Shelf, 2011
Color, 48 pages

Big Mama runs Okie Dokie Donuts, a doughnut shop that offers all kinds of flavors, all made with love. Realizing that she and her clumsy but ever-helpful assistant Henry may not be enough to run a store with such growing popularity, Big Mama considers hiring someone new. Mr. Mayweather, a salesman arrives with a solution: Mr. Baker, an automated robot baking machine. Reluctantly, Big Mama gives the contraption a try, only to have it spew out the most disgusting doughnut flavors. Now, Big Mama must do something-before the robot destroys her store and before the lunch crowd arrives.

Kids who love television cartoons will be drawn to this book with its unusual premise and wacky characters, complete with opening theme song. Eliopoulous balances instantly appealing gross-out humor with just a hint of more adult topics, such as the debate between homemade versus mass-produced food and society's reliance on technology — both subjects that could lead to classroom discussion even for this age group. Eliopoulous' art is unusual and busy, but patient, visual readers will find themselves poring over each page.

EDUCATIONAL TIE-INS:

Food; Technology; Robots

"WHAT'S NEXT ..."

THE MANY ADVENTURES OF JOHNNY MUTTON

Story and art by James Promios

Harcourt, 2001
Color, 48 pages

The same kind of off-the-wall, wacky humor found in Eliopoulous' book is also present in Promios' story of a sheep raised by a human mother. Johnny Mutton is gregarious and odd, especially when he dresses up like a giant runny nose for Halloween. That, along with his other silly antics, will keep kids laughing. Promios' crude and colorful art works with the zany story and will appeal to fans of books by Dav Pilkey.

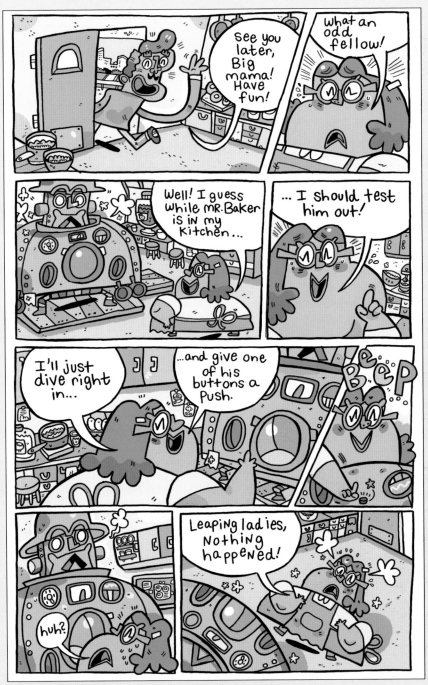

© 2011 Chris Eliopoulous

P.T.A. Night

Story and art by Jeremy Scott

Image/Silverline, 2009
Color, 32 pages

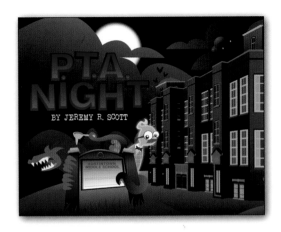

A simple Parent Teacher Association meeting becomes complicated when a host of horror and fantasy creatures show up unexpectedly. Before members of the school staff know what is happening, zombies attack, the janitor turns into a werewolf, an alien arrives because of the science teacher's experiment, a ghost professor appears to teach a silly lesson, and a creature from the deep decides to help out in the cafeteria.

Scott's almost completely wordless graphic novel uses double-page spreads with slight variations on what is happening in each room of a haunted middle school to tell his story. As a wordless story, this book is a great choice for reluctant readers who will develop visual reading skills by paying close attention to small details. The individual stories make excellent writing prompts for teachers and parents who want their children to engage with the story even more. Even though the story uses traditional horror characters, the result is funny, not scary, and Scott's brightly colored digital art gives the book a modern feel, making it a good choice, even for older kids.

EDUCATIONAL TIE-INS:

Storytelling; School; Diorama activity and coloring page available at *http://www.shadowlinecomics.com/Activity-Pages/PTAactivities.pdf*

HEADS UP:

Contains some cartoon violence.

"WHAT'S NEXT ..."

FANG FAIRY

Story and art by Andy J. Smith

Capstone/Stone Arch, 2007
Color, 40 pages

Young readers looking for silly scares will laugh at Jeremy Kreep's attempts to find the hideous beast that stole his little brother's tooth from under his pillow. Smith's wild art has just the right touch of Hollywood ghoulishness to appeal to readers who love the horror-stories-gone-wild aspect of *P.T.A. Night*.

DEAR DRACULA

Story by Joshua Williamson
Art by Vincente Navarette

Image/Silverline, 2008
Color, 48 pages

Children who enjoyed how the supernatural, spooky elements of *P.T.A. Night* are turned from something scary into something funny may enjoy this reinterpretation of a traditional "letters to Santa" story. In this case, a young boy sends a letter to Dracula, hoping his favorite monster will hear his plea and turn him into a real vampire for Halloween.

© 2009 Jeremy R. Scott.

Sam & Friends Mysteries series

Story by Mary Labatt
Art by Jo Rioux

Kids Can Press, 2009-2011
Black and white, 96 pages each

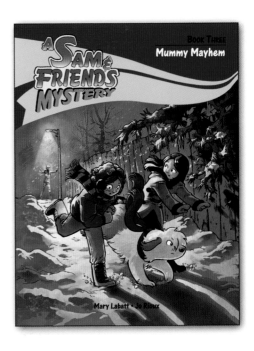

Jennie takes an immediate liking to her new neighbor's female sheepdog, Sam, and soon realizes she can hear the animal's thoughts. Sam reveals to Jennie that she is a detective and loves solving mysteries. Jennie keeps her special connection with Sam secret from everyone but her best friend, Beth, and the three become Woodford's amateur sleuths on the lookout for strange happenings in their small town. Sam's nose for mystery brings them to investigate a reclusive man they're convinced is Dracula, track down an underwater monster while on vacation, search for an escaped ancient mummy from the museum, and determine whether new neighbors are a coven of witches.

Labatt's series of gentle stories features simple plots with mysteries that are solved by the end of each book, reminiscent of the *Bailey School Kids* chapter-book series. Those kids who don't pick up on the formula will enjoy the big reveal at the conclusion of each book; those who do will, nevertheless, be entertained by the sheer silliness. Young readers will easily relate to the trio's overactive imagination. Rioux has appealing art with some manga influences, and her clear storytelling makes this series ideal for newly independent readers. Sam is different from most dogs in stories for this age level — she is snarky and opinionated, creating a perfect balance for the safe, simple plots.

IN THIS SERIES:

Book One: *Dracula Madness*
Book Two: *Lake Monster Mix-up*
Book Three: *Mummy Mayhem*
Book Four: *Witches' Brew*

EDUCATIONAL TIE-INS:

Monsters; Folklore; Imagination; Detectives

"WHAT'S NEXT ..."

THE 3-2-3 DETECTIVE AGENCY: THE DISAPPEARANCE OF DAVE WARTHOG

Story and art by Fiona Robinson

Abrams/Amulet, 2009
Color, 76 pages

Readers who enjoyed the mystery elements of *Sam & Friends* may like this silly story about a group of animals who start a detective agency. Robinson makes more use of the conventions of the mystery genre, and the story is more complex, making this ideal for readers ready for something more sophisticated than Sam's adventures.

Material from *Mummy Mayhem* is used by permission of Kids Can Press Ltd., Toronto. Text © 2010 Mary Labatt.
Illustrations © 2010 Jo Rioux.

Sketch Monsters

Story by Joshua Williamson
Art by Vincente Navarrete

Oni Press, 2011
Color, 40 pages

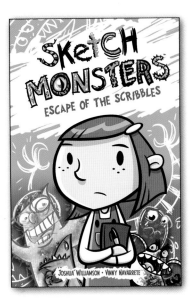

No matter how much she tries, Mandy can't seem to express her emotions, except through her art. But when the monsters she draws in her sketchbook escape and start to cause havoc in the real world, Mandy must capture them by using the emotion each represents.

Even though Williamson's story has an important message about expressing emotions, he wraps it in a cute story that will make sense to young readers, especially those who love to draw and create. Navarrete's art is a bright, colorful mix of cartoonish characters with sharp outlines and monsters who look as if they were drawn by a child. This keeps the tone of the book light and works well with the rollicking chaos caused by Mandy's monsters.

IN THIS SERIES:
Volume 1: Escape of the Scribbles

EDUCATIONAL TIE-INS:
Emotions; Art and artists

HEADS UP:
Contains minor instances of cartoon violence.

"WHAT'S NEXT ..."

NINA IN THAT MAKES ME MAD!
Story by Steven Kroll and Hilary Knight; art by Hilary Knight

Toon Books, 2011
Color, 32 pages

As in *Sketch Monsters*, emotions are the main focus of the story by Kroll and Knight. Since kids get mad when they're told what to do, when they aren't listened to, or when something goes wrong, readers will appreciate Nina's candor, even as they laugh at Knight's retro art and smile at the sweet ending. Nina will help kids better understand their emotions and the proper ways to express them both in the classroom and at home.

MR. MEN AND LITTLE MISS SERIES

LITTLE MISS SUNSHINE: HERE COMES THE SUN!
Story by Michael Daedalus Kenny; art by Victoria Maderna

MR. BUMP: LIGHTS, CAMERA, BUMP!
Story by John Hardman; art by Matthew Britton

Viz, 2012
Color, 80 pages each

The popular *Mr. Men and Little Miss* series of children's picture books (originated by Roger Hargreaves) gets a graphic-novel update for a new generation, with modern references and a few bits of potty humor, but the same classic humor. Children who enjoyed Mandy's wild times with her emotions will also laugh at the silly adventures of Little Miss Sunshine, Mr. Bump, Mr. Grumpy, Little Miss Scary, Mr. Messy, and the rest of the gang in Dillydale.

FANTASY • HUMOR

The Squat Bears series

Story and art by Émile Bravo
Translation by J. Gustave McBride

Yen Press, 2010-2011
Color, 32 pages each

After a hard day's work, all the Squat Bears want to do is eat dinner and go to bed, but, when they get home, they find a tall blonde girl sleeping across all seven of their beds. So they set off to find the giant-slaying prince, still hoping for a good night's sleep in the end. But their troubles are far from over, and soon they have to deal with magic beans, Puss in Boots, enchanted princes, princesses on the run, and a fairy godmother who is sick of being bothered all the time.

Bravo mashes traditional fairytales firmly together, resulting in a fantasyland in which all the familiar characters end up stumbling over one another. Children will love spotting the different tales in their new incarnation, but the real joy lies in watching the bears' consternation and frustration with everyone around them. Bravo sticks to rectangular panels, making the story easy to follow, even for young comics readers, and his thinly lined art allows his characters to show a wide range of emotions. The story has many puns, making this not only a good pick for readers who are ready for chapter books, but also for older readers who still love fairytales.

IN THIS SERIES:

Goldilocks and the Seven Squat Bears
The Hunger of the Seven Squat Bears
Beauty and the Squat Bears

EDUCATIONAL TIE-INS:

Fairy tales

HEADS UP:

Contains very minor instances of kissing.

"WHAT'S NEXT ..."

THERE'S A WOLF AT THE DOOR: FIVE CLASSIC TALES
Story by Zoë B. Alley
Art by R.W. Alley

Roaring Brook Press, 2008
Color, 40 pages

THERE'S A PRINCESS IN THE PALACE: FIVE CLASSIC TALES
Story by Zoë B. Alley
Art by R.W. Alley

Roaring Brook Press, 2008
Color, 40 pages

Fairytale fans will enjoy more mash-ups in these two picture-book graphic novels. Each oversized page is packed with fun details and humorous asides. The Alleys tie traditional fairytales together, just as Bravo does, but in a way that carries the characters — and their readers — through the five stories in each volume. Together with *Squat Bears*, these two books are a great addition to classroom studies of classic tales, offering students a way to see how the stories can be altered and combined to create new works.

Goldilocks and the Seven Squat Bears first published in France under the title: *Boucle d'or et les sept aux ours nains* © Editions du Seuil, 2004; *Beauty and the Seven Squat Bears* first published in France under the title: *La Belle aux ours nains* © Editions du Seuil, 2009

Squish series

Story by Jennifer L. Holm
Art by Matthew Holm

Random House, 2011-2012
Black and white with green, 96 pages each

Squish is an amoeba who goes to school, hangs out with his friends, Peggy and Pod, and enjoys comic books — especially ones starring his favorite super-hero, Super Amoeba. But when Squish and his friends encounter the amoeba bully Lynwood in detention, he threatens to consume Peggy unless Squish helps him cheat on an upcoming test. In the second volume, it's a new school year, and Squish is tired of Peggy and Pod and hopes to make newer, cooler friends. When the Algae brothers arrive, Squish tries his best to impress them.

The Holms combine an unusual story concept with a likeable underdog character to create an offbeat, hilarious series that explores such school issues as friendships, peer pressure, bullying, and cheating. Squish's super-hero role model often provides him with guidance to handle these issues, giving readers positive messages. Using a simple art style with bold lines, lots of white space, and green highlights that add to its slimy appeal, the series should attract reluctant readers. Using the books' text-filled arrows, readers learn more about each character, laugh at the sarcastic remarks about what's happening in the story, and discover scientific information about amoebas, paramecia, algae, slime molds, planaria, and more. Additional science and drawing activities are included at the end of each book.

IN THIS SERIES:

No. 1: *Super Amoeba*
No. 2: *Brave New Pond*
No. 3: *The Power of the Parasite*

EDUCATIONAL TIE-INS:

Microbiology; Amoebas; Peer pressure; Bullying (*Super Amoeba*)

HEADS UP:

Contains some instances of name-calling.

"WHAT'S NEXT ..."

DRAGONBREATH SERIES
Story and art by Ursula Vernon

A full list of titles appears on Page 221.

Penguin/Dial Books, 2009-2011
Black and white with green, 208 pages each

Vernon's part-graphic novel, part-prose series about a young dragon deals with school issues — including a nasty Komodo dragon bully — and strange adventures as well as his inability to breathe fire. It will appeal to readers who enjoy the same underdog spirit found in *Squish*. Both series features similar bold art and black, white, and green color schemes that will appeal to boy readers.

"Book Cover," © 2011 by Random House Children's Books, from *Squish: Super Amoeba Book 1* by Jennifer L. Holm and Matthew Holm. Used by permission of Random House Children's Books, a division of Random House, Inc. Interior illustration from *Squish: Brave New Pond Book 2* by Jennifer L. Holm and Matthew Holm, © 2011 by Jennifer Holm and Matthew Holm. Used by permission of Random House Children's Books, a division of Random House, Inc.

Stinky

Story and art by Eleanor Davis

Toon Books, 2008
Color, 40 pages

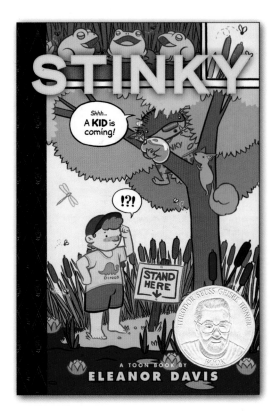

Stinky the Ogre lives in a mucky swamp, where he enjoys pickled onions and spending time with his giant toad, Wartbelly. Only one thing bothers Stinky — children — because he thinks they love to take baths and eat apples and don't like worms or slugs. When a boy named Nick starts building a tree house in Stinky's swamp, the ogre makes plans to stop him.

Young readers will laugh out loud at Davis' clever story, which seamlessly pairs a fantasy creature with the real world. Stinky's attempts to scare off Nick are harmless, and, by the time the two realize that they should be friends, readers will be cheering for them. The text is simple enough for emerging readers, and Davis' bright art uses simple lines to build a detailed (but never busy) portrait of the swamp. Both boys and girls should enjoy this fun tale.

AWARDS:
2009 Association for Library Service to Children Theodore Seuss Geisel Honor; 2009 Association for Library Service to Children Notable Children's Book

EDUCATIONAL TIE-INS:
Friendship; First impressions; Lesson plans available at *http://www.toon-books.com/lp_stinky.php*; Read online in English, French, Spanish, Russian, and Chinese: *http://toon-books.com/rdr_two.php#stinky*

"WHAT'S NEXT ..."

HARVEY COMICS CLASSICS VOLUME ONE: CASPER THE FRIENDLY GHOST
Edited by Leslie Cabarga
Story and art by various creators

Dark Horse, 2007
Black and white with some color, 480 pages

This collection of classic Casper comics from the early 1950s to the mid-1960s is a reversal from Davis' story: Casper tries to make new friends without scaring them, while Stinky *wants* to scare people. Nevertheless, it still explores the same concepts — of first impressions, being misunderstood, and the importance of friendship — in a gentle and charming way.

Super Diaper Baby series

Story and art by Dav Pilkey

Scholastic/Blue Sky Press, 2002; 2011
Black and white, 128 pages and 192 pages

When George and Harold find themselves in detention, they decide to pass the time creating graphic novels starring the hero Super Diaper Baby. In one adventure, a baby is dunked into super-power juice that Deputy Dangerous extracted from Captain Underpants, hoping to steal his abilities. Instead, Deputy Dangerous' further experiments transform him into a piece of poop. With a new robot ant creation, Super Diaper Baby must defeat the villain before he destroys the city. In another adventure, Dr. Dilbert Dinkle is mistakenly shot with a ray that transforms him into liquid. When his thirsty cat Petey drinks the doctor, he is reborn as a puddle of pee and decides to steal all the toilets in the city. Super Diaper Baby must defeat Dr. Dinkle before he destroys the city.

Both Super Diaper Baby graphic novels are companion books to Pilkey's wildly popular and controversial *Captain Underpants* series. These comics reflect the sensibility of the two boys — Super Diaper Baby's creators — and are rife with spelling mistakes, silly story logic, strange references, and crude drawings. The appeal is that young readers are aware of the joke and know how ridiculous these stories are. Pilkey's flip-o-rama feature is a silly take on traditional flip books, giving the series an interactive element and reinforcing the sense of parody. Packed with potty humor, these books have strong appeal to both boys and reluctant readers.

IN THIS SERIES:

The Adventures of Super Diaper Baby
Super Diaper Baby 2: The Invasion of the Potty Snatchers

EDUCATIONAL TIE-INS:

Heroes; Parody

HEADS UP:

Contains multiple instances of potty humor and some cartoon violence.

"WHAT'S NEXT ..."

THE ADVENTURES OF OOK AND GLUK: KUNG-FU CAVEMEN FROM THE FUTURE

Story and art by Dav Pilkey

Scholastic/Blue Sky Press, 2010
Black and white, 176 pages

George and Harold's other graphic novel, produced between the two Super Diaper Baby books, is a departure with fewer potty references but just as much humor. Two cavemen must travel into the future to learn kung fu in order to take down their cruel village chief, who is receiving help from his resourceful and equally cruel descendant.

Adventures in Cartooning series

Story and art by James Sturm, Alexis Frederick-Frost, and Andrew Arnold

First Second, 2009; 2010
Color, 112 pages (Adventures in Cartooning)
Black and white, 80 pages (Activity Book)

When a knight is convinced that a dragon has kidnapped the princess, the Magic Cartooning Elf appears to help him. The elf promises to aid the knight in finding the dragon but only if he can tell the knight about comics and cartooning along the way. Traveling from the top of a mountain to the depths of the sea and finally into the dragon's lair, the elf tells the knight all about how to create comics, using panels, doodles, and both word and thought balloons. Then, when the knight is upset by a rainy day, the elf takes him on another quest to practice all his cartooning skills and, hopefully, find a way to stop the rain.

Using the framework of a silly story, readers are introduced to basic cartooning concepts including panels, gutters, and word and thought balloons, along with how to use lines and symbols to show movement, mood, or emotion and how basic shapes can be used to create characters. Simple art conveys clear instructions, and the story is entertaining but does not overshadow the various lessons. Recap pages at the end reinforce the lessons learned. The workbook companion is equally entertaining and provides a variety of exercises in drawing faces and objects, using backgrounds to create perspective, story sequencing, and more, with each task moving the story along.

IN THIS SERIES:

Adventures in Cartooning:
How to Turn Your Doodles into Comics
Adventures in Cartooning Activity Book

AWARDS:

ALSC Notable Children's Book; CCBC Choice (University of Wisconsin); NYPL Book for Reading and Sharing; Booklist Top 10 Graphic Novel for Youth; Booklist Top Ten Art Book for Kids; Library Media Connection Best of the Best; Illinois Bluestem Book Award Master List; Indiana Young Hoosier Award Master List; Rhode Island Children's Book Award Master List; Vermont Dorothy Canfield Fisher Award Master List

EDUCATIONAL TIE-INS:

Cartooning; Creativity; Art and artists

"WHAT'S NEXT ..."

COMICS TO GO: 19 STORIES FOR YOU TO FINISH AND MORE
Story and art by Mike Herrod

Blue Apple Books, 2008
Color, 64 pages

For aspiring cartoonists who want more practice, this book provides single prompts to complete, including drawing scenes, character design, creating backgrounds, and more. The end of the book provides additional prompts to create full comics along with blank comics panel templates.

ADVENTURE • HISTORICAL FICTION • HUMOR

Adventures of Rabbit and Bear Paws series

Story by Christopher Meyer and Chad Solomon
Art by Chad Solomon

Little Spirit Bear Productions, 2006-2012
Color, 32 pages each

Brothers Rabbit and Bear Paws are two Ojibwa brothers living in 18th century colonized North America with their family. Hyperactive Rabbit and naive Bear Paws love playing pranks using their father's spirit powder that allows them to transform into animals for short periods of time. The brothers' love of mischief sends them on adventures and often gets them into trouble, such as when they try to prevent a conflict between the British and the French, accompany their father's friend on a fur-trading expedition, unexpectedly participate in a competition for a young woman's hand in marriage, tell false stories about a giant stealing from the tribe, and anger a healer who uses his talents for the wrong reasons.

Possibly one of the only current graphic representations of Native North Americans as primary characters, this series offers information on 18th century history and Native North American culture, traditions, and legends in a fun, light story. Young readers will identify with Rabbit and Bear Paws and their love of pranks and enjoy the snappy dialogue, which is kid-authentic, even though the series is set in the past. Each volume explores traditional Anishinabek teachings without being preachy, making the series a good choice for character education units. Solomon's art is full of action, physical humor, and sight gags that depict the playful antics of these characters in a way that readers will fully enjoy.

IN THIS SERIES:

A full list of titles appears on page 222.

EDUCATIONAL TIE-INS:

North American history – 18th Century; Native North American myths and legends; Native North American culture and customs; Character education; Family; Fur trade; Lacrosse (*The Voyageurs*)

HEADS UP:

Contains some instances of cartoon violence.

"WHAT'S NEXT ..."

ASTERIX SERIES
Story by René Goscinny
Art and story by Albert Uderzo

A full list of titles appears on page 222.

Orion, 2004-2011
Color, 48-56 pages

Readers will recognize Asterix and Obelix (originated in 1959) and their hilarious adventures as the inspiration for Rabbit and Bear Paws. This classic European comics series contains the same buddy-comedy elements set in a historical time period: in this case Gaul, in 50 B.C. during Roman rule. Goscinny and Uderzo's stories lean heavily on satire but also feature the same kind of fun as in the tales of Solomon and Meyer.

© 2006–2012 Christopher Meyer and Chad Solomon.

18

Amazing Greek Myths of Wonders and Blunders

Story and art by Michael Townsend

Dial Books for Young Readers, 2010
Color, 160 pages

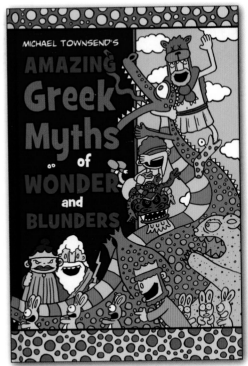

© 2010 Michael Townsend

Back before there were pants or toasters or tractors, there were the Greek Gods, and they had lots of adventures, most of which involved fighting, helping humans who were forced to go on quests, making half-human/half-god babies, or punishing humans who did stupid things. From Zeus and his jealous wife, Hera, to the half-god Hercules and his daring deeds, to the boastful Arachne, this collection retells favorite myths with plenty of focus on the humor.

Townsend's anthology is the perfect choice for kids who love foolish characters and silly action. Focusing on the kid-appropriate mythological elements (especially when they can be played for humorous effect, such as Midas' inability to eat when he turns all his food to gold), Townsend sharply downplays the sexual components of the classics. The typical violence of these stories, while present, is mostly off-page and used for humor — Hercules' murder of his family happens behind blacked-out panels marked "Censored! Censored!" Less well-known tales, such as that of Pyramus and Thisbe, sit comfortably alongside such better-known stories as that of Pandora. The bold, crayon colors of Townsend's art bring the vacant eyes and dopey grins of his characters to vivid life.

EDUCATIONAL TIE-INS:
Greek mythology

HEADS UP:
Contains some cartoon violence (some visible, some hidden by other art), some death, and minor instances of kissing.

"WHAT'S NEXT ..."

PIRATE PENGUIN VS. NINJA CHICKEN: TROUBLES WITH FRENEMIES
Story and art by Ray Friesen

Top Shelf, 2011
Color, 96 pages

Pirate Penguin and his sometime friend Ninja Chicken love to fight but they will take a break for smoothies or silliness. Friesen's collection of comic shorts isn't as over-the-top nutty as Townsend's work, but it shares the same zany take on the world. The bright art and bizarre cast of characters will have kids chuckling as they read.

Chi's Sweet Home series

Story and art by Konami Kanata
Translation by Ed Chavez

Vertical, 2010-2012
Color, 152-168 pages

When a little kitten is separated from her mother and siblings, she doesn't know how to get home. Luckily, a human family rescues her and gives her a new home. Now, the kitten (named "Chi" by the family's young son) has to learn many new skills, including how to use a litter box, how to survive a trip to the veterinarian, how to navigate a staircase, and how to make friends.

Kanata turns the simple, realistic story of owning a pet into a sweet, compelling series. Readers will be eager to follow along on Chi's latest adventure, laughing as she makes mistakes and smiling when she does something adorable. Even though readers know what Chi is thinking, she still thinks and acts like a cat, not a person. Kids will laugh at the mild potty humor, including references to "chi" or urine, after which the family's son accidentally names their new pet. Readers who aren't comfortable with reading Japanese comics that have been printed right-to-left will be happy that the publisher has "flipped" *Chi's Sweet Home* to make it easier on North American audiences.

IN THIS SERIES:

A full list of titles appears on page 225.

EDUCATIONAL TIE-INS:

Pet ownership and care; Paper crafts available at *http://www.chisweethome. net/fun/*

HEADS UP:

Contains very minor potty humor.

"WHAT'S NEXT ..."

ONE FINE DAY SERIES
Story and art by Sirial
Translation by JuYoun Lee

A full list of titles appears on page 225.

Yen Press, 2010
Black and white, 160-176 pages

Readers who like such heartwarming pet stories as *Chi's Sweet Home* will appreciate the sweetness of Sirial's fantasy-tinged stories about the puppy Nanai, the kitty Guru, and the mouse Rang who live in a magical village. The thinly lined art sometimes depicts the pets as animals and sometimes as little children.

HUMOR • SCHOOL & FAMILY

HUMOR • SCHOOL & FAMILY

Amelia Rules! series

Story and art by Jimmy Gownley

Simon & Schuster/Atheneum, 2003-2011
Color, 160-192 pages

After Amelia's parents divorce, she and her mother move to a small town to live with her Aunt Tanner, a former rock star who turned her back on fame. Amelia's new friends are an unusual group: Pajamaman only wears pajamas and doesn't talk; Reggie is obsessed with super-heroes; and Rhonda is obsessed with Reggie. With her friends, Amelia fights evil ninjas, tries to survive insane teachers, and learns the true meaning of "sneeze-barf." But at the same time she finds out what it really means to be a friend and that her family will always be there for her, even when she is at her most annoying.

Amelia and her friends face a host of such serious issues as divorce, poverty, parents deployed in the military, and life-threatening illness, while coping with the usual pre-teen concerns about school, puberty, cliques, bullying, friendship, and more. Gownley keeps these real-world problems from overwhelming his characters by tempering them with plenty of action and humor. He uses a wide variety of art styles, font choices, and bright colors, all of which keep readers' eyes glued to the page. The characters are realistically imperfect, which only makes them more appealing.

IN THIS SERIES:
A full list of titles appears on page 224.

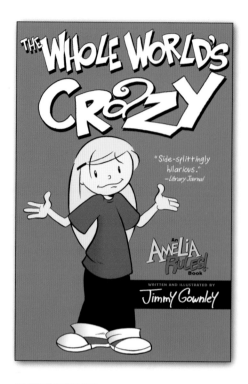

EDUCATIONAL TIE-INS:
Divorce; Self-esteem; Friendship; Family; Teaching guide available at *http://series. simonandschuster.net/Amelia-Rules!*

HEADS UP:
Contains multiple instances of cartoon violence, some potty humor, hints at strong language, and some name-calling.

"WHAT'S NEXT ..."

***ODDLY NORMAL* SERIES**
Story and art by Otis Frampton

VOL. 1: ODDLY NORMAL
VOL. 2: FAMILY REUNION

SLG Publishing, 2006-2007
Color, 112-128 pages

Amelia Rules fans looking for another fish-out-of-water tale will enjoy the story of Oddly Normal, a young half-witch who doesn't fit into either the human world or the fantasy one of Fignation.

© 2006-2011 Jimmy Gownley

Chicagoland Detective Agency series

Story by Trina Robbins
Art by Tyler Page
Lettering by Zack Giallongo

Lerner/Graphic Universe, 2010-2011
Black and white, 64 pages each

When Megan, the new girl in town, wants to buy a pet that won't aggravate her father's allergies, she ends up in a pet-food store, where she meets the store owner's son, Raf. Soon, the haiku-writing, manga-reading, vegetarian teams up with the anti-social computer genius, along with a talking dog the two rescue from a lab, to solve strange crimes in their town. The Chicagoland Detective Agency is on the case to investigate students turned zombies, an emo rock star who might have stolen a mummy, and a mysterious pack of dogs.

Both paranormal fans and mystery readers should enjoy Robbins' series. Megan and Raf are cool enough to appeal to young readers wanting to read about teenagers, but none of their exploits are overly violent or scary. Page's art is bold, firmly standing on the line between detailed and cartoonish, giving readers lots to look at in each panel. The supplemental information at the ends of the books gives readers more insight into each character and the monsters they face down.

IN THIS SERIES:

#1: The Drained Brains Caper
#2: The Maltese Mummy
#3: Night of the Living Dogs

EDUCATIONAL TIE-INS:

Animal testing; Poetry; Mummies
(*#2: The Maltese Mummy*)

HEADS UP:

Contains some cartoon violence.

"WHAT'S NEXT ..."

SCARED TO DEATH SERIES
Story by Virginie Van Holme; art by Mauricet; color by Laurent Carpentier; translation by Luke Spear

#1: THE VAMPIRE FROM THE MARSHES
#2: MALEVOLENCE AND MANDRAKE

Cinebook, 2008-2009
Color, 48 pages each

Readers ready for a touch more paranormal in their reading might enjoy the adventures of best friends Robin and Max. The two boys first find themselves the target of a group of local vampires; then, they must look into the disappearance of a classmate, which might be related to the new girl in school and a coven of witches.

LEAVE IT TO CHANCE SERIES
Story by James Robinson
Art by Paul Smith

A full list of titles appears on page 224.

Image, 2002-2003
Color, 112 pages each

Robinson's series about an eager adventurer named Chance Falconer who goes against the wishes of her father, a famous occult investigator, to help solve supernatural crimes in her city features both the paranormal and the mystery elements found in Robbins' series. Even though the series is darker in tone, it is still a lot of fun and age-appropriate for middle-grade readers.

Cowa!

Story and art by Akira Toriyama
Translation by Alexander O. Smith

Viz, 2008
Black and white with 16-page color insert,
208 pages

When best friends Paifu (half vampire, half were-koala) and Jose (a ghost) arrive at school one evening to a nearly empty classroom, they discover their town is suffering from fatal monster flu. With the only cure in the hands of a witch at the top of a mountain, Paifu and Jose set off with Paifu's rival Arpon and Maruyama, an ex-sumo wrestler and the only human living in the town, on a deadly quest to save the others. On their way, the group encounters thieves, gangsters, and finally a monster who guards the woods at the base of the witch's mountain.

Toriyama uses many elements that made his classic series *Dragon Ball* an appealing series for boy readers: simple, iconic art; lively action sequences; extended fight scenes; and sight gags with an occasional fart joke. *Cowa* also features a significant amount of violence: Maruyama and other villains use guns, and one of the kid monsters is accidentally shot in the hand but heals quickly. To offset the amount of violence, this book has strong messages about friendship, teamwork, and dealing with differences.

EDUCATIONAL TIE-INS:

Friendship; Teamwork; Vampires; Quest stories

HEADS UP:

Contains realistic and cartoon violence, multiple instances of potty humor, and some name-calling. Story reads right-to-left.

"WHAT'S NEXT ..."

BEET THE VANDEL BUSTER SERIES

Story by Riku Sanjo
Art by Koji Inada

A full list of titles appears on page 225.

Viz, 2004-2007
Black and white, 184-216 pages

Readers who enjoy the adventure and high action in *Cowa* may be ready to try this series about an enthusiastic, yet sometimes overly eager, young monster hunter on a quest to rid the land of demon-like creatures called Vandels. Though not as cute as *Cowa*, this series has its share of laughs.

Cowa! © 1997 by Bird Studio/Shueisha Inc.

Elephants Never Forget series

Story and art by Bill Slavin

Kids Can Press, 2011
Color, 80 pages

When Otto (a sensitive elephant) discovers that his best friend, Georgie (a monkey), has been kidnapped, he is devastated. Otto's friend Crackers (a parrot) convinces him to sneak onto a plane to head to the United States, where they believe the mysterious Man with the Wooden Nose has taken George. Trying their best to remain inconspicuous, the pair are ignored by everyone in New York City, until they visit the zoo. At the zoo, the pair meet Smiling Sam, an alligator who assures them that his friends will know where Georgie is. Unknowingly, Otto and Crackers become involved with members of New York's seedy alligator underworld, who use the two friendly animals for their own selfish purposes.

Kids will love the silly characters throughout this book, from Otto and Crackers (absurdly ignored by everyone around them) to the trio of alligators, including the accented wrestling champion Cajun Joe, the rapping Shorty Pants, and crime boss Big Al. Readers paying extra attention to this part lighthearted romp, part mystery caper, may figure out that Georgie is actually Curious George. Slavin's art has a classic style with lots of details and sight gags. There are many opportunities for laughs, especially with a large elephant as a main character — such as when Otto stops the subway with his rear, tries to squeeze himself into taxi cabs and portable toilets, or has explosive peanut-allergy sneezes. With its open-ended conclusion, readers can look forward to more adventures with this hilarious duo.

IN THIS SERIES:

#1: *Big City Otto*

EDUCATIONAL TIE-INS:

Friendship; New York City

HEADS UP:

Contains minor instances of cartoon violence.

"WHAT'S NEXT ..."

SPIRAL-BOUND

Story and art by Aaron Renier

Top Shelf, 2005
Black and white, 144 pages

While three animal friends each work on a project over summer break, they attempt to solve the mystery of the monster that lives in their town's pond. Readers who like the idea of animals having silly adventures, as in *Elephants Never Forget*, will enjoy Renier's highly detailed art, which brings his animal world to life.

THE MUPPET SHOW SERIES

Story by Roger Langridge
Art by Roger Langridge and Amy Mebberson

A full list of titles appears on page 226.

Boom! Studios, 2009-2011
Color, 112-128 pages

Readers who have finished *Big City Otto* and find themselves looking for more stories with zany animal characters, lots of laughs, and a bit of befuddling mystery should try Roger Langridge's *Muppet Show* graphic novels, perfect for both those who know the characters already and those who are being introduced for the first time.

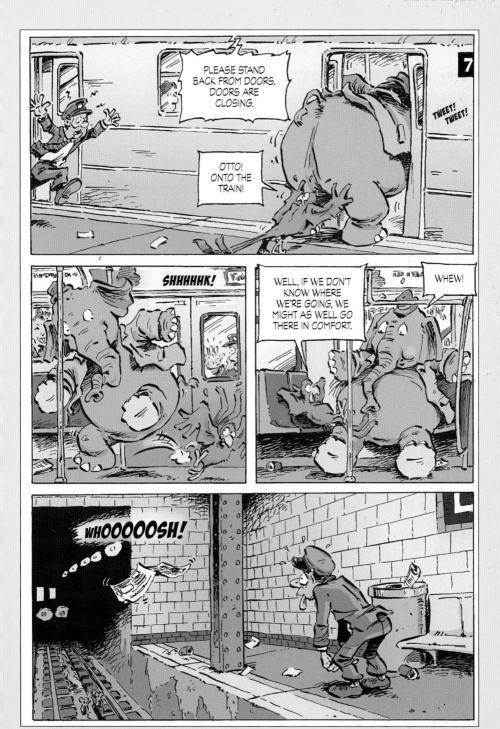

The ElseWhere Chronicles series

Story by Nykko
Art by Bannister
Colors by Corentin Jaffré

Lerner/Graphic Universe, 2009-2011
Color, 48 pages each

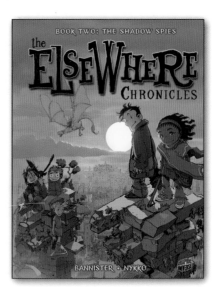

While exploring the old house of her recently deceased grandfather, Rebecca and her new friends Max, Theo, and Noah find a movie projector that opens a doorway into another world. After being attacked by a strange shadow creature, Rebecca and Max find themselves trapped in ElseWhere, hoping that Theo and Noah can reopen the portal. Eventually, Theo and Noah join the others in ElseWhere and learn that Rebecca's grandfather has visited this other world and hidden other portals across the land. The four set out to find the portals in order to return home, while avoiding the shadow creatures that are controlled by the Master of Shadows, who has a curious interest in both Rebecca and the portals to our world.

Using a story structure similar to the *Chronicles of Narnia*, this series doesn't shy away from intensity and dire situations in the characters' desperate search to find a way home. Readers who like more thrills in their fantasy will enjoy the increasingly dangerous threats and the intense cliffhanger endings of this series. This intensity extends to the backstories of the characters, as readers are introduced to Max's abusive family and given hints concerning Rebecca's violent experiences in Rwanda. Bannister's art is playful but maintains the series' dark mood while immersing readers in the fantastic landscapes of Elsewhere.

IN THIS SERIES:

A full list of titles appears on page 226.

AWARDS:

2007 Lyon Festival Youth Prize (French editions)

EDUCATIONAL TIE-INS:

Friendship; Family; Quest stories; Adoptive children; Abuse; Children of war

HEADS UP:

Contains instances of realistic violence, mature themes, and death.

"WHAT'S NEXT ..."

VERMONIA SERIES

Story and art by Yoyo

A full list of titles appears on page 226.

Candlewick, 2009-2012
Black and white, 208 pages each

In this manga series, four teens are swept into Vermonia, a world torn by warfare, where they struggle to control and wield the powers given to them by their animal guardians in order to save the people they meet. Readers who like stories of ordinary humans ending up in strange new worlds, such as *ElseWhere*, may like the kid-friendly action, romance, and fantasy of *Vermonia*.

G-Man series

Story and art by Chris Giarrusso

Image, 2009-2010
Color, 96 pages and 128 pages

Mikey, also known as G-Man, finally achieves super-powers, when he cuts up his family's magic carpet to make a cape. But his bullying older brother David wants to get in on the action and, using the remnants of the blanket, is soon flying the skies as Great-Man. Together, the two must face super-villains, stupidity, the collision of multiple universes, and a dangerous destabilization of magic that only they can fix.

Using conventional super-hero elements, Giarrusso creates his own world: one that simultaneously pokes fun at super-hero comics and celebrates them. With child characters that are droll and often aware of the idiocy of the world around them, Giarrusso plays up such elements up for comic effect. There is a lot of fighting, but no one is ever seriously injured. Both the story and his art are reminiscent of those in Bill Watterson's *Calvin and Hobbes* comic strip, making this a great pick for boys who might shy away from other reading material.

IN THIS SERIES:

#1: Learning to Fly
#2: Cape Crisis

EDUCATIONAL TIE-INS:

Sibling relationships

HEADS UP:

Contains multiple instances of cartoon violence and name-calling.

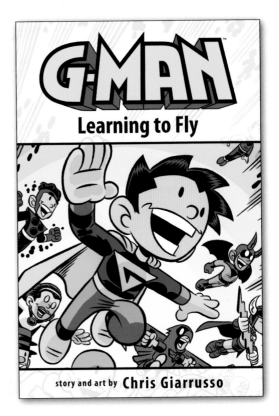

"WHAT'S NEXT ..."

FRANKLIN RICHARDS SERIES
Story by Chris Eliopoulos with Marc Sumarek
Art by Chris Eliopoulos
**FRANKLIN RICHARDS: SON OF A GENIUS
ULTIMATE COLLECTION BOOK 1
FRANKLIN RICHARDS: SON OF A GENIUS
ULTIMATE COLLECTION BOOK 2**

Marvel, 2010
Color, 184 pages and 216 pages

Franklin Richards is the high-spirited, trouble-making son of Reed and Sue Richards of The Fantastic Four. Despite the best efforts of robot nanny H.E.R.B.I.E., Franklin ricochets from one hilarious disaster to another, making this series perfect for *G-Man* fans who love chaos and silliness.

Graphic Guide Adventures series

Story by Liam O'Donnell
Art by Mike Deas

Orca Books, 2007-2011
Color, 64 pages each

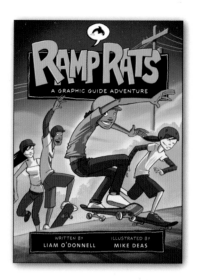

In this set of interconnected stories, a group of friends find themselves in the middle of perplexing mysteries and must use information they've learned to help solve them. Siblings Nadia and Devin learn to survive in the wild in order to expose a corrupt bureaucrat, uncover a scheme to sabotage Nadia's all-girl soccer team, and discover a corporation's plans to control the nation's food supply. Friends Bounce and Pema, while enjoying the skateboard park, discover vandalism that threatens local businesses and try to expose crooked land developers using a video posted online. All four friends, along with Marcus, Bounce's stepbrother, meet at a global leaders summit and uncover a plot to prevent Marcus' father from delivering a speech about the importance of restricting corporations in the sale of fresh water.

Packaged as an engaging mystery series with a diverse cast of characters, these books integrate instructional information into well-written stories without being overbearing. O'Donnell selects such appealing topics as survival skills, soccer, and skateboarding but also includes such socially minded subjects as media literacy and food sustainability. The book focusing on government is a good supplement to curriculum, and, though the book is set in Canada, the information isn't specific to the country. These books tend to be text-heavy, but the non-fiction elements, fast pace, clean art, and strong storytelling are sure to appeal to reluctant readers.

IN THIS SERIES:

A full list of titles appears on page 227.

EDUCATIONAL TIE-INS:

Survival skills; Environmentalism (*Wild Ride*); Skateboarding; Public space (*Ramp Rats*); Soccer; Teamwork (*Soccer Sabotage*); the Media; Advertising; Reporters; the Internet (*Media Madness*); Food chain; Nutrition; Agriculture (*Food Fight*); Government; Politics; Democracy (*Power Play*)

HEADS UP:

Contains some instances of realistic violence and death.

"WHAT'S NEXT ..."

HOWTOONS: THE POSSIBILITIES ARE ENDLESS!

Story by Saul Griffith and Joost Bonsen
Art by Nick Dragotta

HarperCollins, 2007
Color, 112 pages

Readers who want more graphic novel, non-fiction fun as is found in the instructional portions of O'Donnell's series, should check out *Howtoons*. Sibling inventors Celine and Tucker show readers how to make their own marshmallow shooter, tree swing, flute, and more while teaching them scientific and engineering principles and workshop safety.

Happy Happy Clover series

Story and art by Sayuri Tatsuyama
Translation by Kaori Inoue

Viz, 2009-2010
Black and white, 192 pages each

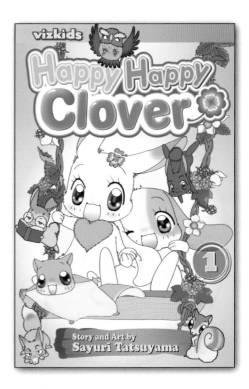

Clover, a happy-go-lucky bunny, lives with her mom and dad in Crescent Forest. Together with her bunny friends — the shy Mallow, the bookish Shallot, and the loyal Kale — Clover plays, goes to school, and runs the Bunny Express postal service. Life in Crescent Forest is happy, even when the annoying fox Cinnamon causes trouble or when Professor Hoot assigns too much homework, but Clover still dreams of the day when she can travel the world with the rambling rabbit, Rambler.

Clover and her friends will appeal to girls, who will understand the animals' desire for independence, their dreams of the future, and their struggles to make friendships work. Light touches of romance, a good dose of silliness, and a lot of sweet sentiment might make this series too sugary for adults, but young readers will be eager to read all the way to the final chapter, which nicely wraps up the characters' stories. Tatsuyama's art is as cheery as her tale, filled with bright sparkly eyes, happy grins, and tears that are quickly soothed. There is a very mild fantasy element, but the focus is mostly on the fun.

IN THIS SERIES:
A full list of titles appears on page 227.

EDUCATIONAL TIE-INS:
Friendship

HEADS UP:
Contains some cartoon violence and very minor kissing. Story reads right-to-left.

"WHAT'S NEXT ..."

FAIRY IDOL KANON SERIES
Story and art by Mera Hakamada
Translation by M. Kirie Hayashi

A full list of titles appears on page 228.

Udon Entertainment, 2009-2010
Black and white, 200 pages each

Happy Happy Clover readers who want more sweet, cheery, all-girl manga fun should look for Hakamada's series about three friends who long to be musical stars — and the fairy princess who helps them achieve their dreams.

Happy Happy Clover © 2006 Sayuri Tatsuyama

Knights of the Lunch Table series

Story and art by Frank Cammuso

Scholastic/Graphix, 2008-2011
Color, 128-144 pages

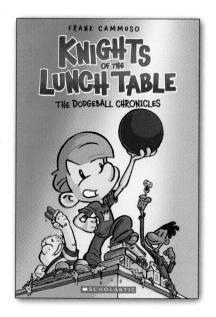

Artie King, the newest student at Camelot Middle School, quickly gets himself in the bad books of Mrs. Dagger, the school's cruel, strict principal. Luckily, he finds fast allies with a trio of fellow students — Percy, Wayne, and Gwen — along with the sage science teacher, Mr. Merlyn. When Artie unlocks a legendary locker that no other student has been able to open, he is deemed the chosen one of Camelot but at the same time becomes an enemy of The Horde, a group of bullies led by Joe Roman. Artie and his friends must fend off the attacks of The Horde, when they are challenged to a dodgeball game, participate in a tournament of battling robots, and rock out during a battle of the bands.

Readers with an interest in legends or mythology will get a kick out of this reimagining of King Arthur in a familiar school setting, which presents such obvious characters as Merlin but also such obscure ones as the three witches and The Lady of the Lake. Regular school situations are raised to silly legendary levels, providing lots of laughs to all readers, even those without an interest in the Arthurian references. Cammuso creates likeable characters who remain true to themselves while dealing with adversity. Positive messages about fairness, determination, and teamwork are authentic without being heavy-handed. Art is colorful and accessible, skilfully depicting both the strong character moments and the silly action sequences.

IN THIS SERIES:

A full list of titles appears on page 228.

EDUCATIONAL TIE-INS:

Legends; King Arthur; Mythology; Bullying; Friendship

HEADS UP:

Contains some instances of name-calling.

"WHAT'S NEXT ..."

WORLD OF QUEST SERIES

Story and art by Jason T. Kruse

VOLUME 1
VOLUME 2

Yen Press, 2007-2008
Color, 144 pages each

Readers who enjoyed the fantasy element of Cammuso's kid version of King Arthur may want to try this series about a young prince who must enlist the help of a square-jawed, stubborn warrior to help rescue his father. Kruse's series features more action and edgier humor but is a good companion to *Knights of the Lunch Table*.

FANTASY · SCHOOL & FAMILY

Little Vampire

Story and art by Joann Sfar

First Second, 2008
Color, 96 pages

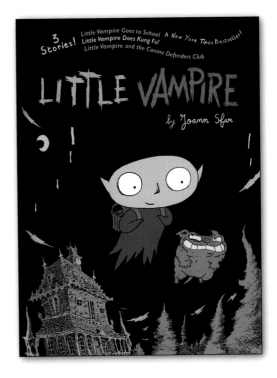

Bored and with no other children to play with, Little Vampire surprises his supernatural family when he asks to attend school. His mother reluctantly agrees, but, when Little Vampire and his dog Phantomato arrive at the school in the middle of the night, they are surprised to see no children. Little Vampire writes in a notebook belonging to a human boy named Michael, and the two become friends. Little Vampire brings his new friend to meet the Captain of the Dead and introduces him to Rabbi Solomon, who teaches the boy kung fu to protect himself against a bully. Then, the two friends rescue a trio of dogs from an animal-testing lab.

Readers who enjoy tales of ghosts, vampires, and other supernatural characters will enjoy Sfar's stories, which walk the line between scary and silly. Sfar touches on such serious topics as death, religion, and the dark impulses that children often have, but balances them with the sweetness of the friendship between Little Vampire and Michael and their message of tolerance, as well as instances of dark humor, such as when Michael's bully is eaten by monsters and thrown up in pieces. Sfar's art is highly detailed and creates a vivid supernatural world. The use of smaller series of panels makes this a book for seasoned graphic-novel readers.

EDUCATIONAL TIE-INS:

Friendship; Bullying; Dogs; Folklore

HEADS UP:

Contains some instances of name-calling, cartoon violence, and potty humor.

"WHAT'S NEXT ..."

SCARY GODMOTHER

Story and art by Jill Thompson

Dark Horse, 2010
Color, 192 pages

Nervous about trick-or-treating with her mean cousin Jimmy on Halloween, Hannah meets Scary Godmother and her monster friends and learns that Halloween and monsters can be fun. Readers who love *Little Vampire*'s blend of scary and silly will enjoy this collection of all four brightly painted *Scary Godmother* stories in an edition that includes many entertaining extras.

Missile Mouse series

Story and art by Jake Parker

Scholastic/Graphix, 2009-2010
Color, 168 pages and 176 pages

While he is usually a solo agent, Missile Mouse's reckless behavior forces his commanders to saddle him with subordinates, first another agent and then a team of security 'bots. With this unwanted support, Missile Mouse attempts to recover a long-lost doomsday machine and the kidnapped genius scientist who is being forced to fix it. Then, he must free a planet full of aliens forced into slavery, while facing down the forces of the Rogue Imperium of Planets and the assassin Blazing Bat.

Parker's stories about a mouse space agent who is part Captain Kirk of *Star Trek* and part Han Solo of *Star Wars* are packed with science-fiction action. Readers who want traditional space drama — complete with dual agents, strange aliens, bizarre scientific devices, and life-or-death choices — will love *Missile Mouse*. Parker's bright art is kid-friendly and has the appeal of a Saturday morning cartoon but never sacrifices the story by being cheesy or campy. There are laser guns blazing, a lot of fighting, and one desperate sacrifice, but both kids and adults who love old-fashioned science-fiction adventures will love Parker's take on the genre.

IN THIS SERIES:

The Star Crusher
Rescue on Tankium3

EDUCATIONAL TIE-INS:

Sacrifice; Slavery (*Rescue on Tankium3*)

HEADS UP:

Contains instances of realistic violence and death.

"WHAT'S NEXT ..."

STAR WARS ADVENTURES SERIES
Stories and art by various creators

HAN SOLO AND THE HOLLOW MOON OF KHORYA
PRINCESS LEIA AND THE ROYAL RANSOM
LUKE SKYWALKER AND THE TREASURE OF THE
    DRAGONSNAKES
THE WILL OF DARTH VADER
BOBA FETT AND THE SHIP OF FEAR
CHEWBACCA AND THE SLAVERS OF THE
    SHADOWLANDS

Dark Horse, 2009-2011
Color, 72-80 pages

Readers who want more science-fiction action with a heart will enjoy these stories that detail episodes from the lives of the characters in the *Star Wars* movies. With only a bit of background from the original *Star Wars* trilogy needed to understand the stories, readers will appreciate the drama, adventure, and thought-provoking themes of this series.

Ninja Baseball Kyuma series

Story and art by Shunshin Maeda

Udon, 2009-2010
Black and white, 200 pages each

For 400 years, Kyuma, a boy ninja, has trained in the mountains, waiting for the call of duty. When Kaoru, team captain of the Moonstar Baseball Club, searches for a solution to its losing streak, he discovers Kyuma and convinces him to join the team. A bit out of touch with the modern world and with no clue how to play baseball, Kyuma tries his best to please his teammates. After a couple of games, he begins to understand the game and his new friends see his potential. But Kyuma's ninja master decrees that he must win *every* game, or he cannot play baseball ever again. The team sets out to win the Platinum Ball Cup, playing against a determined all-girls team, a team that uses dirty tricks, and a highly experienced team, all of which underestimate Kyuma and his team's ninja baseball skills.

This series combines high action, sports, and humor making it a perfect title to attract reluctant boy readers. Much of the humor comes from Kyuma's boy-out-of-time status — he is clueless about the game of baseball, he refers to his team captain as "my liege," and he speaks in silly formal dialogue. Kyuma manages to convey positive messages in a way that is both honest and endearing, teaching readers the importance of focusing on fun rather than winning, the value of teamwork and friendships, and the way that working hard can lead to success. While the ninja element plays a minor role in this series, it may be enough to appeal to young readers who are not yet ready for such more mature series as *Naruto*.

IN THIS SERIES:

A full list of titles appears on page 229.

EDUCATIONAL TIE-INS:

Baseball; Teamwork; Friendship; Ninjas

HEADS UP:

Contains some instances of cartoon violence and minor potty humor. Story reads right-to-left.

"WHAT'S NEXT ..."

WHISTLE SERIES

Story and art by Daisuke Higuchi

A full list appears on page 229.

Viz, 2004-2010
Black and white, 200-208 pages

When soccer-lover Sho finds a middle school with a team that will let him play despite his short stature, his new teammates mistake him for a soccer phenom. Now, he must improve or quit the team. Higuchi's series is appropriate for younger readers who like *Ninja Baseball Kyuma's* themes of teamwork and determination, but it will also appeal to older sports fans.

Pilot and Huxley series

Story and art by Dan McGuiness

Scholastic/Graphix, 2011
Color, 64 pages each

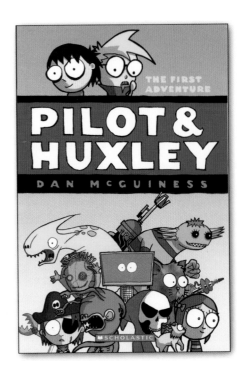

When best friends Pilot and Huxley forget to return a videogame on time, alien creatures send The Reaper to retrieve it in order to get the activation codes for their newest weapon to enslave the planet. The Reaper zaps the two boys to another dimension, where they must retrieve a golden nose hair in order to be sent back to Earth. Unfortunately, things don't quite go as planned, and the two boys (with their shape-shifting friend Brett) end up in Christmas Land. There, they must fight a twisted elf and a Rudolph who has been laser-equipped by an evil Santa Claus.

With its *South Park*-style randomness and humor, McGuiness' story of the inter-dimensional adventures of two boys is sure to attract reluctant readers. With a good dose of gross-out humor including references to pee, butts, snot, farts, and boogers, this series has the edgy appeal of many adult cartoons without going over the offensive edge. There is plenty of kid-appropriate stuff that boys will love, including robots, video games, aliens, zombies, transforming pirates, and futuristic weapons. Guiness' art is bold and colorful and his dialogue rings true.

IN THIS SERIES:

The First Adventure
The Next Adventure

EDUCATIONAL TIE-INS:

Aliens; Holidays; Time travel; Friendship

HEADS UP:

Contains some instances of cartoon violence and potty humor.

"WHAT'S NEXT ..."

PINKY AND STINKY
Story and art by James Kochalka

Top Shelf, 2002
Black and white, 208 pages

Pinky and Stinky's mission to be the first pig astronauts to visit Pluto goes wrong, and they crash-land on the moon, where they are caught between hot-headed American astronauts and aliens who become unexpected friends. Kochalka's story isn't as gross as McGuiness', but they share similar randomly wacky science-fiction plots.

DALEN AND GOLE: SCANDAL IN PORT ANGUS
Story and art by Mike Deas

Orca Books, 2011
Color, 128 pages

When two alien friends find a tunnel that leads to a small fishing town on Earth, they uncover a plot to deplete the town's fish population in order to produce overpriced fuel on their own world. Deas' story may not have quite the same edgy quality as *Pilot and Huxley*, but it possesses the same spirit of friendship and a similar offbeat story with science-fiction elements.

ADVENTURE • FANTASY • ROMANCE

Rapunzel's Revenge series

Story by Shannon and Dean Hale
Art by Nathan Hale

Bloomsbury, 2008-2010
Color, 144 pages each

Rapunzel grows up thinking she's the daughter of the witch Mother Gothel, but, when she discovers the truth — that she was stolen from her mother as a baby — Gothel traps her in a prison tree for four years. After training herself to use her increasingly long hair as a whip, Rapunzel escapes and, with the help of a boy named Jack, she decides to bring down Gothel and then the giant Blunderboar. But Jack has his own tricky past, which has caught up with him and may get in the way of his happiness with Rapunzel.

Teen fantasy writer Hale and her husband blend two classic fairy tales — "Rapunzel" and "Jack and the Beanstalk" — with the Wild West and a touch of steampunk, resulting in a girl-power story with plenty of action, humor, fantasy, and romance. Nathan Hale (no relation) brings the stories to life with a vivid color palette, lots of details, and an art style that makes even the fairy-tale creatures seem realistic.

IN THIS SERIES:

Rapunzel's Revenge
Calamity Jack

AWARDS:

2009 Young Adult Library Services Association Great Graphic Novel for Teens List (*Rapunzel's Revenge*); 2009 Association for Library Service to Children Notable Children's Book (*Rapunzel's Revenge*); 2010 Young Adult Library Services Association Popular Paperbacks: Twists on the Tale List (*Rapunzel's Revenge*); 2011 Young Adult Library Services Association Great Graphic Novel for Teens List (*Calamity Jack*)

EDUCATIONAL TIE-INS:

Wild West; Retellings; Fractured fairy tales; Teacher's guides available at *http://www. squeetus.com/stage/Rapunzel_TG.pdf* (*Rapunzel's Revenge*) and *http://www. squeetus.com/stage/CalJack_TG.pdf* (*Calamity Jack*); Paper dolls available at *http://spacestationnathan.com/ rapunzelpaperdolls.pdf*

HEADS UP:

Contains multiple instances of realistic violence and some kissing.

"WHAT'S NEXT ..."

WONDERLAND
Story by Tommy Kovac
Art by Sonny Liew

Disney Press, 2008
Color, 160 pages

Kovac takes the already off-kilter story of Alice in Wonderland and turns it on its head by focusing instead on Mary Ann, the White Rabbit's cleanliness-obsessed maid. Readers who love seeing stories from new perspectives, such as the Hales' two books, will enjoy the oddness, fantasy, and humor in *Wonderland*, especially as illustrated in Liew's crazed cartoon style.

From *Rapunzel's Revenge* by Dean and Shannon Hale. Copyright © 2008 by Dean and Shannon Hale. Reprinted by permission of Bloomsbury Publishing, Inc. All rights reserved.

Robot City Adventures series

Story and art by Paul Collicutt

Candlewick/Templar, 2009-2010
Color, 48 pages each

In Robot City, men and women live peacefully together with robots, but that doesn't mean that all is quiet. While the Coast Guard keeps watch over the port, detectives Rod and Mike try to stop a dangerous rust epidemic. Meanwhile, scientist Sarah Cross must rescue the historic Metal Men, and train conductor Harrison has to solve a murder on board his train.

Collicutt's retro series will remind adults of older comics both in story and in art, while kids will love the fully realized world of humans and robots. His stories are full of adventure and bravery but are all-inclusive, featuring characters of both genders and many races. There is fighting and one murder, but nothing too graphic for young readers. The occasionally challenging vocabulary and subtle humor make this series a better choice for upper-elementary-school students.

IN THIS SERIES:

#1: City in Peril!
#2: Rust Attack!
#3: The Indestructible Metal Men
#4: Murder on the Robot City Express

EDUCATIONAL TIE-INS:

Coast Guard (*City in Peril*); Detectives (*Rust Attack* and *Murder on the Robot City Express*); Inventors (*The Indestructible Metal Men*)

HEADS UP:

Contains some realistic violence and death.

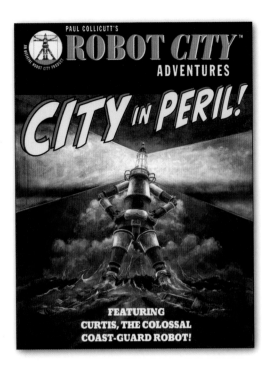

"WHAT'S NEXT …"

JOEY FLY, PRIVATE EYE SERIES

Story by Aaron Reynolds
Art by Neil Numberman

VOLUME 1: CREEPY CRAWLY CRIME
VOLUME 2: BIG HAIRY DRAMA

Henry Holt Books for Young Readers, 2009-2010
Color, 96-128 pages

Readers who like the retro feel of *Robot City Adventures* but who want more humor will like Reynolds' *noir* detective story set in a city populated by insects. Numberman's cartoonish art brings Joey Fly and his scorpion assistant Sammy Stingtail to hilarious life, leaving readers chuckling at the slightly gross humor and the silly mysteries.

The Indestructible Meta Man. Copyright © 2010 by Paul Collicutt. Reproduced by permission of the publisher, Candlewick Press, Somerville, MA.

Robot Dreams

Story and art by Sarah Varon

First Second, 2007
Color, 208 pages

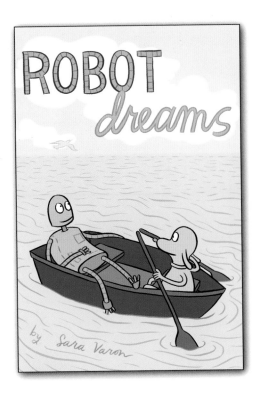

Dog makes himself a robot friend, but, after a trip to the beach and a swim in the ocean, Robot rusts in place on a beach towel. Dog sadly leaves his friend behind, and the two spend the next year apart: Robot dreaming of being free, as Dog tries to find another friend.

Robot Dreams is a melancholic look at the end of a relationship. Though older readers may view Varon's almost-wordless story as the break-up of a romantic relationship, younger readers who see friendships come and go will also understand the pain of parting and the healing that allows people to move on. Varon's deceptively simple art depicts cartoonish characters drawn with a few thin lines and colored in a soft palette. This simplicity, as well as her gentle storytelling and her use of animals as stand-ins for humans, make this a graphic novel that can — and will — speak to readers across a wide range of ages.

AWARDS:

2008 Young Adult Library Services Association Great Graphic Novel for Teens List; 2008 Association for Library Service to Children Notable Children's Book

EDUCATIONAL TIE-INS:

Friendship

HEADS UP:

Explores the concept of death through metaphor.

"WHAT'S NEXT ..."

THE CLOUDS ABOVE
Story and art by Jordan Crane

Fantagraphics, 2005
Color, 224 pages

Observant readers of *Robot Dreams* will spot Robot reading a copy of *The Clouds Above*, a story about a little boy and a large cat who are late for school and, instead of being caught by their mean teacher, decide to ascend to the clouds through a staircase to the sky. This book's all-ages appeal makes it a nice fit with Varon's tale.

BAKE SALE
Story and art by Sara Varon

First Second, 2011
Color, 160 pages

When Eggplant offers his friend Cupcake the chance to travel to Europe with him, Cupcake works hard to earn the money selling his baked goods, only to have to choose between his dream and his friendship. Though *Bake Sale* is not wordless, as *Robot Dreams* is, it has the same sweet art and tone and it includes recipes for the goodies that Cupcake makes.

WORDLESS

Salt Water Taffy: The Seaside Adventures of Jack and Benny series

Story and art by Matthew Loux

Oni Press, 2008-2011
Black and white, 72-96 pages

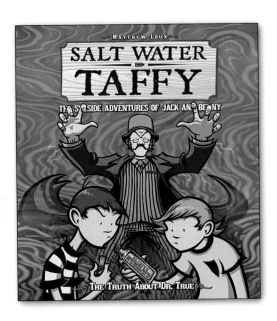

Moving with their parents for the summer to the small town of Chowder Bay, Maine, brothers Jack and Benny are convinced they're in for a summer of boredom. It turns out that Chowder Bay has more than its share of adventures, including a Civil War-era ghost returning to find his murderer, a sea monster who forces lobsters to steal taffy, a giant eagle who loves hats, Dan the ever-hungry wolf, and, of course, the seagulls.

This modern-day collection of tall tales is told through the eyes of two typical boys with whom readers will easily identify. Loux adds plenty of dry humor to his series, as the boys and the adults around them accept the oddities of Chowder Bay as if they are perfectly normal. Readers will love the realistic sibling relationship, which involves some arguing but mostly a lot of fun, since the boys don't have other kids to play with. Loux' art features thick black lines with sharp edges in a hip, modern style, which adds even more fun.

IN THIS SERIES:

#1: *The Legend of Old Salty*
#2: *A Climb up Mt. Barnabas*
#3: *The Truth about Dr. True*
#4: *Caldera's Revenge, Part I*
#5: *Caldera's Revenge, Part II*

EDUCATIONAL TIE-INS:

Maine; Local history; Sibling relationships; Tall Tales

HEADS UP:

Contains some cartoon violence and death.

"WHAT'S NEXT ..."

SHADOW ROCK

Story and art by Jeremy Love and Robert Love

Dark Horse, 2006
Color, 80 pages

Readers who like the seaside small-town setting and fantastic adventures of *Salt Water Taffy*, but who want a little more horror, should look for *Shadow Rock*. When Timothy moves to Shadow Rock, he doesn't fit in because he's from the city and because he's black. But he soon makes a new friend: a ghost who needs Timothy to solve the mystery of who killed him years before.

Sardine in Outer Space series

Story by Emmanuel Guibert; art by
Joann Sfar (Books One to Four)
Story and art by Emmanuel Guibert
(Books Five and Six)

First Second, 2006-2008
Color, 96-128 pages

With her friend Little Louie, Sardine
explores the galaxy on her uncle's
spacecraft, *The Huckleberry*, meeting
different aliens, some of whom turn out to
be friends and others, dangerous and silly
enemies. Sardine's uncle, the space pirate
Captain Yellow Shoulder, and his crew
have two main foes: Supermuscleman,
dictator of the universe, and his mad-
scientist sidekick Doc Krok. Those
evildoers want to brainwash all the
children of the universe to make them
obedient. Sardine and her friends stay one
step ahead of the villains and manage to
save the children from those evil plans in
fun, silly ways.

Packed with crude humor and sarcastic
wit, this series offers readers a collection
of silly stories that will appeal to both boys
and girls. Sardine is a capable, resourceful
main character, and her supporting cast is
equally interesting. Guibert sets up a never-
ending battle of wits between Sardine
and her friends and Supermuscleman that
capture the spirit of childhood pranks and
will leave readers laughing through all six
volumes. Cleverly self-aware, *Sardine in
Outer Space* also includes elements readers
will love: pirates, aliens, and intergalactic
adventure. The use of slapstick violence
inches toward the extreme at times, but the
series maintains a light, fun tone.

IN THIS SERIES:

A full list of titles appears on page 231.

EDUCATIONAL TIE-INS:

Pirates; Space; Aliens; Satire

HEADS UP:

Contains some instances of potty humor, some
cartoon violence, and minor adult alcohol use.

"WHAT'S NEXT ..."

KAPUT AND ZOSKY

Story and art by Lewis Trondheim

First Second, 2008
Color, 80 pages

Kaput and Zosky are two alien would-be world
conquerors who can never seem to get it right.
Readers who enjoy *Sardine* will recognize the
same kind of sarcastic, dry humor and the similar
bumbling antics between these two strange aliens
as exist between Supermuscleman and Doc Krok.

The Secret Science Alliance and the Copycat Crook

Story and art by Eleanor Davis

Bloomsbury, 2009
Color, 160 pages

Genius Julian Calendar hopes to shed his nerdy image when he starts a new school, but it doesn't take long for him to be labeled a loser again. Accidently revealing his high intelligence in class, Julian receives a coded letter that leads him to meet other unexpected science geeks: Greta (a branded troublemaker) and Ben (the school's star jock). The three form The Secret Science Alliance and begin working together on projects and recording them in The Invention Notebook. But, when the notebook goes missing and an article in the paper reveals a new invention by Dr. Stringer, one of Julian's heroes — an invention that looks a lot like one of Ben's ideas — the three friends vow to stop the rogue scientist.

Davis' book about science geeks, both the obvious and the not-so-obvious, is a tribute to all readers who have ever felt different or out of place. This book can be used to teach kids about the empowerment that comes with strong friendships and how often the very thing that makes one an outsider can be used in positive ways. Davis' bold, colorful art features an incredible amount of detail, which readers will pore over. She successfully incorporates science into the structure of the story using schematics, blueprints, flow charts, and cross sections in the panel and page layouts. These diagrams often reveal interesting details about each of the main characters, giving them even more depth and interest.

EDUCATIONAL TIE-INS:

Inventions; Science; Geeks; Friendship; Bullying

"WHAT'S NEXT ..."

MAL AND CHAD SERIES
Story and art by Stephen McCranie

THE BIGGEST, BESTEST TIME EVER! FOOD FIGHT!

Philomel, 2011-2012
Color, 224 pages each

Mal is an elementary-school genius, but his only friend is his talking dog, Chad. In a series of adventures that will appeal to *Calvin and Hobbes* fans as well as those who love the geek-power theme of *Secret Science Alliance*, Mal and Chad build a rocket ship, travel in time and in Chad's dreams, and try to catch the eye of Megan, Mal's crush.

From *Secret Science Alliance and the Copycat Crook* by Eleanor Davis. Copyright © 2009 by Eleanor Davis. Reprinted by permission of Bloomsbury Publishing, Inc. All rights reserved.

Sidekicks

Story and art by Dan Santat

Scholastic/Arthur Levine Books, 2011
Color, 224 pages

When a severe peanut allergy prevents middle-aged Captain Amazing from protecting the city from harm, he decides it's time to find a new sidekick to offer super-hero support. The Captain's pets — Roscoe, a dog; Fluffy, a hamster; and Shifty, a chameleon — each want the position. However, since his previous sidekick, Manny (aka Static Cat), ran away, the super-hero states: *No pets*. Roscoe feels he's ready to impress his master, but Fluffy has no real super-powers, so he seeks out the runaway Manny for training. When one of Captain Amazing's enemies emerges from hiding using powers stolen from others, all four animals must team up to defeat him without Captain Amazing's help.

Santat's super-hero pet story has both visual appeal and humor and will capture the interest of readers with its animated-movie-style quality. His colorful art skillfully depicts the cuteness of the various pet animals, as well as moodier scenes and displays of over-the-top super-heroics. The story is straightforward but includes clever subplots and flashbacks, which add depth for those readers looking for a story with more weight. Combining great comic-book action with lots of heart, Santat's *Sidekicks* features positive messages — including determination, brains over brawn, and using strengths to overcome adversity.

EDUCATIONAL TIE-INS:

Family; Friendship; Pets; Heroes

HEADS UP:

Contains minor instances of realistic violence.

"WHAT'S NEXT …"

SCRATCH9 SERIES
Story by Rob M. Worley
Art by Jason T. Kruse and Mike Kunkel

VOLUME 1: THE PET PROJECT

Ape Entertainment, 2011
Color, 100 pages

When stray cat Scratch finds himself a test subject of the dastardly Dr. Schrodinger, he is left with the ability to summon the spirit of each of his nine lives and decides to use this power to fight evil. Readers who love the antics and emotional impact of the animal super-heroes of *Sidekicks* will also enjoy *Scratch9*.

Text and illustrations © 2011 by Dan Santat.

The Smurfs series

Story by Yvan Delporte, Gos, and Peyo
Art by Peyo and Gos

Papercutz, 2010-2011
Color, 56-64 pages

Soon after Peewit finds a magical flute that can make people dance when played, it is stolen by a man who wants to use the flute's powers for his own selfish purposes. Peewit and his friend Johann visit a wizard hoping for guidance on recovering the flute. The wizard sends the two to find the Smurfs — small, blue magical creatures — for help. Hidden from humans, Smurfs work hard and celebrate their accomplishments. Often their leader, Papa Smurf, must help the other Smurfs out of dangerous situations, such as finding a cure to a bug bite that turns Smurfs mean and purple, undoing the out-of-control wishes of a magical egg, scolding an ambitious Smurf who unfairly rules the village in Papa's absence, and protecting the village from the schemes of the evil wizard Gargamel.

This classic European series that inspired the 1980s cartoon includes elements of fantasy and adventure, but readers will likely be drawn to the madcap humor. The relationships between Smurfs echo sibling relationships, and readers will enjoy the laughs as the characters argue with, play pranks on, and otherwise annoy each other. With the help of Papa Smurf, these conflicts are always resolved, though they do come with consequences. This series will complement classroom units on community and the importance of teamwork. The use of the Smurf language is a perfect tie-in to lessons on nouns and verbs. Readers will find their favorite Smurf among the wide group of archetypal characters, from the know-it-all Brainy to the prankster Jokey.

IN THIS SERIES:

A full list of titles appears on page 232.

EDUCATIONAL TIE-INS:

Community; Responsibility; Teamwork

HEADS UP:

Contains minor instances of cartoon violence and name-calling.

"WHAT'S NEXT ..."

MOOMIN SERIES

Story and Art by Tove Jansson and Lars Jansson (Book Six)

A full list of titles appears on page 233.

Drawn and Quarterly, 2006-2011
Black and white, 88-128 pages

Smurfs readers will find the same whimsical sense of humor in Jansson's collection of comic strips about a family of hippo-like trolls. The misadventures of the Moomins are more easygoing and gentle and lack the more traditional fantasy elements of *The Smurfs*, but readers will still find much to enjoy.

Smurfs and the Magic Flute and Purple Smurf © 2010 Peyo Licensed through Lafig Belgium; English translation © 2010 Papercutz

Three Thieves series

Story and art by Scott Chantler

Kids Can Press, 2010-2011
Color, 112 pages each

Dessa, a 14-year-old orphan, arrives in Kingsbridge, the royal city, with her traveling-circus companions Topper (a juggler) and Fisk (a strong man). Hoping to find clues to the whereabouts of her missing twin brother, Dessa is, instead, coerced into a plot by her two friends to rob the queen's royal treasure. When the heist fails, the three become fugitives on the run from the queen's guard while searching for the queen's missing chamberlain — who, Dessa believes, is the mysterious man who kidnapped her brother years ago.

With a strong female lead character — Dessa is spunky, resourceful, and intelligent — Chantler's fast-paced, action-heavy adventure series has strong appeal to both boys and girls. He balances the dramatic plot with humor, including witty dialogue, slapstick comedy, and great comic relief on the part of both Fisk and Topper. Chantler provides a tale of intrigue, capturing readers' attention by slowly revealing characters' backstories. The fantasy element of the series is understated, allowing the pure adventure to come through. His art is clean and bright, but moody when needed; his storytelling is clear, making this a great series for reluctant and struggling readers.

IN THIS SERIES:

Tower of Treasure
The Sign of the Black Rock

AWARDS:

2011 Joe Shuster Award
(*Tower of Treasure*)

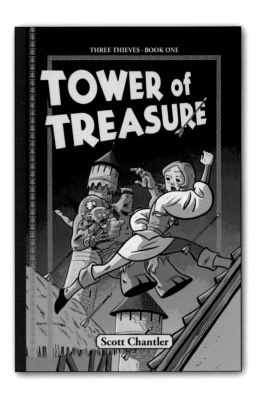

THREE THIEVES · BOOK ONE

TOWER of TREASURE

Scott Chantler

EDUCATIONAL TIE-INS:

Friendship; Family; Middle Ages

HEADS UP:

Contains some instances of realistic violence and adult alcohol use.

"WHAT'S NEXT ..."

ALISON DARE SERIES
Story by J. Torres
Art by J. Bone

LITTLE MISS ADVENTURES
THE HEART OF THE MAIDEN

Tundra, 2010
Black and white, 96-104 pages

Readers looking for another series with a strong female lead as capable and smart as Dessa may enjoy *Alison Dare*. This daughter of an archaeologist and a super-hero has her parents' adventurous spirit and drags her two friends on exciting, yet often perilous, exploits.

Tiny Tyrant series

Story by Lewis Trondheim
Art by Fabrice Parme
Translation by Alexis Siegel

First Second, 2007
Color, 64 pages each

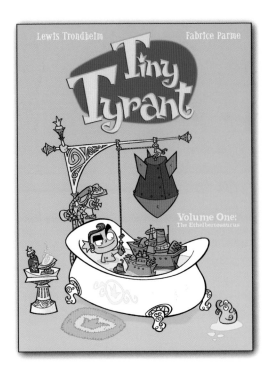

Ethelbert is a 6-year-old king who is demanding, impulsive, and spoiled — and rules Portocristo on his terms only. He is constantly looking for bigger and better ways to satisfy his own wants, as well as to outshine his royal cousin Sigimund and impress Princess Hildegardina, who has more wealth than both cousins combined. Guidance from his prime minister and his personal tutor rarely discourage him from his grandiose demands. These include cloning a dinosaur and sending it back in time to be named after him, replacing all the children in the kingdom with robot versions of himself, and declaring war on America for material worth documenting by the newly appointed royal biographer.

Trondheim has created a hilarious character in Ethelbert, presenting his adventures in a series of short comics. Young readers will laugh at his ridiculous demands and spoiled-brat behavior and might even see a bit of themselves in his antics. While Ethelbert has free rein to do as he pleases, these stories are usually cautionary tales, often with consequences of the king's demands. The series has references to poop, burps, and farts but also features video games, dinosaurs, racing cars, and lasers. Parme's illustrations lack panel borders, but his clear storytelling skills, highly detailed art, and amusing sight gags will appeal to all readers.

IN THIS SERIES:

Volume One: The Ethelbertosaurus
Volume Two: The Lucky Winner

EDUCATIONAL TIE-INS:

Royalty; Kings; Power; Responsibility; Rivalry

HEADS UP:

Contains some instances of potty humor.

"WHAT'S NEXT ..."

PRINCESS AT MIDNIGHT
Story and art by Andi Watson

Image, 2008
Black and white, 64 pages

Fans of Ethelbert's hilarious demands will see the same kind of over-the-top behavior in this tale of a girl who commands a kingdom after she goes to sleep at night. Watson's story looks at many of the same themes as in *Tiny Tyrant* — such as rivalry between relatives — with the same kind of laughs.

HUMOR

37

To Dance: A Ballerina's Graphic Novel

Story by Siena Cherson Siegel
Art by Mark Siegel

Simon & Schuster/Atheneum, 2006
Color, 64 pages

Siena always wanted to dance. When she was 6, she started ballet classes in her native Puerto Rico. When she was 9, she saw the Bolshoi Ballet perform and knew that she wanted to be a ballerina. By the time she was 11, she was studying at The School of American Ballet in New York City. Her life was filled with blisters, school, performances, injuries, and fighting parents, all the while with a commitment to dance.

Whether or not readers have studied dance, they will be intrigued by Siegel's story of growing up in the ballet world, from the joy she feels while dancing to the pain and hardships that ballet forces upon her. Siegel's husband illustrates this memoir with realistic images that seamlessly flow into one another and are bordered by delicate details that bring to life both the ballets being performed and the more mundane life of a dance student. Set in the 1970s and 1980s, this story has a timeless quality that will speak to any readers who dream of a life of beauty and art.

AWARDS:

2007 Association for Library Service to Children Notable Children's Book; 2007 Association for Library Service to Children Robert F. Siebert Award Honor

EDUCATIONAL TIE-INS:

Ballet; Careers

"WHAT'S NEXT ..."

LILY RENÉE, ESCAPE ARTIST: FROM HOLOCAUST SURVIVOR TO COMIC BOOK PIONEER

Story by Trina Robbins
Art by Anne Timmons and Mo Oh

Lerner/Graphic Universe, 2011
Color, 96 pages

Robbins' biography of Renée, who escaped the Holocaust before finally landing in America working as a comic-book illustrator, is more serious and less fanciful than Siegel's flowing memoir. But readers who like reading about young women overcoming odds to find work in the arts will appreciate both Renée's story and the supplemental materials at the end of the book.

MEMOIR

Wizard of Oz series

Story by L. Frank Baum; adapted by Eric Shanower; art by Skottie Young; colors by Jean-Francis Beaulieu

Marvel, 2009-2011
Color, 192-200 pages

When a tornado strikes her Kansas farm, Dorothy is swept away from her aunt and uncle and thrown into the magical land of Oz. A host of new friends, including The Cowardly Lion, The Scarecrow, and The Tin Man, help her search for a way home. But even after she finds one — no thanks to The Wizard — the adventures in Oz continue, as The Tin Man and The Scarecrow, with unexpected help from a boy named Tip, face a rebellion in Emerald City. Then, finding her way to Oz again through a storm at sea, Dorothy must work with her friends to free an imprisoned queen and her children.

Shanower's adaptation of Baum's children's fantasy series keeps all the fun of the original books, though children who have only seen the movie versions of the first and third novels may be surprised by how much Hollywood changed. There is a lot of nonsense, making this best for readers who like their books to have some oddness, but Baum also plays around with such weighty topics as gender issues, family dynamics, and death. Even though these stories feature many strong female characters, Young's art is not light and girly. Boys should also be drawn to these fantasies, especially because they feature some action and a lot of humor.

IN THIS SERIES:

A full list of titles appears on page 234.

AWARDS:

2010 Will Eisner Comic Industry Awards for Best Publication for Kids and Best Limited Series or Story Arc

EDUCATIONAL TIE-INS:

Quest stories; Friendship

HEADS UP:

Contains minor instances of cartoon violence and death of a non-human character.

"WHAT'S NEXT ..."

LITTLE ADVENTURES IN OZ SERIES
Story and art by Eric Shanower

A full list of titles appears on page 234.

IDW, 2010
Color, 136 pages each

Shanower began his work with Oz by creating tales that continue the adventures of Ozma, Dorothy, The Scarecrow, and other fantastic creatures of Baum's wondrous land. Though reminiscent of the work of John R. Neill, the original Oz artist after the initial novel, Shanower's realistic art has its own modern feel, which breathes life into these fantasies.

BARON: THE CAT RETURNS
Story and art by Aoi Hiiragi

Viz, 2005
Black and white, 224 pages

Readers who want another tale of a girl flung into a magical world should read Hiiragi's story about a girl named Haru who rescues a cat, not knowing he is a prince, and then finds herself in the land of cats, betrothed to the prince in thanks for her service. Young romantics, cat lovers, and fans of strong female characters will enjoy this tale.

Yotsuba&! series

Story and art by Kiyohiko Azuma
Translation by Amy Forsyth (Vols. 1, 4-9);
Stephen Paul (Vols. 2-3)

Yen Press, 2009-2011
Black and white, 192-224 pages

Yotsuba (her name means "four-leaf," as in a clover) is a green-haired 5-year-old who moves to a small Japanese city with her adoptive father, Koiwai. They become friends with their new neighbors, Mr. and Mrs. Ayase and their daughters Asagi, Fuuya, and Ena — and Yotsuba quickly ropes everyone into her adventures. As an excitable, naive young girl, she often misunderstands events — from visiting a farm to learning about recycling to just enjoying an ice cream — with hilarious results.

Each chapter in Azuma's graphic novel features Yotsuba interacting with — and often misunderstanding, Amelia Bedelia-like — a different person or concept. The title *Yotsuba&!* is pronounced "Yotsubato," meaning "Yotsuba and …" Chapter one is "Yotsuba and Moving," chapter two is "Yotsuba and Greetings," and so on. As a young girl, Yotsuba finds all events new, and her stories are a terrific way for readers to learn about Japanese culture with the help of translator's notes in the margins. *Yotsuba&!* reads right-to-left, but even readers new to manga will be able to follow Azuma's art, which combines realistic settings with cartoon characters.

IN THIS SERIES:

A full list of titles appears on page 235.

AWARDS:

2006 Japan Media Arts Festival Excellence Prize in Manga; 2008 Young Adult Library Services Association Great Graphic Novel for Teens List (Volume four); 2007 Young Adult Library Services Association Popular Paperbacks: What's So Funny? List

EDUCATIONAL TIE-INS:

Japanese culture; Adopted families

HEADS UP:

Contains multiple instances of cartoon violence and name-calling. Story reads right-to-left.

"WHAT'S NEXT …"

LITTLE LULU SERIES

Story and art by John Stanley and Irving Tripp

A full list of titles appears on page 235.

Dark Horse, 2005-2011
Black and white (Vol. 1-18), Color (Vol. 19-29), 200-240 pages

Lulu, created by Marjorie Henderson Buell as a panel-cartoon character in the 1930s, is as outgoing and exuberant as Yotsuba, and her comic-book adventures have the same timeless humor. Dark Horse has released 29 volumes of Little Lulu stories in addition to several collections of her friends' comics.

Yotsuba&! © Kiyohiko Azuma / YOTUBA SUTAZIO

Zita the Spacegirl series

Story and art by Ben Hatke

First Second, 2011
Color, 192 pages

Zita and her friend Joseph find a fallen asteroid with a mysterious device inside. When Zita pushes the button on the device, Joseph is sucked into a hole in space. To save him, Zita must find the courage to travel light-years across the universe, traverse a doomed alien world, and face down a group of mystics who believe that Joseph is the only one who can save them from destruction.

Hatke's graphic novel combines the best elements of hard science fiction, fantasy quest tales, and gentle friendship stories. Zita is spunky but remains a believable little girl. Her determination to find Joseph and her ability to see the best in others draws a host of alien creatures and robots to her and inspires them to help her. Hatke uses thin ink lines and a muted color palette to build a highly detailed world that readers will want to linger over, picking out the many different creatures Zita passes. There are fighting and many tense moments, but the heart of the story is sweet and touching, sure to appeal to fans of adventure, science fiction, and strong girls.

IN THIS SERIES:

Book One: Far from Home

EDUCATIONAL TIE-INS:

Friendship; Sacrifice; Quest stories

HEADS UP:

Contains minor instances of realistic violence.

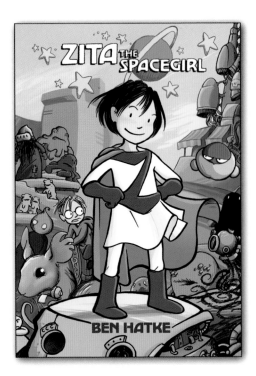

"WHAT'S NEXT ..."

KORGI SERIES
Story and art by Christian Slade

A full list of titles appears on page 236.
Top Shelf, 2007-2011
Black and white, 80-96 pages

Readers who love Hatke's soft art and strong female lead should enjoy Slade's mostly wordless fantasy series about a young "Mollie" named Ivy and her "Korgi" pup Sprout. They face down dangers together, using wits, wings, and Sprout's still-growing powers.

SWANS IN SPACE SERIES
Story and art by Lun Lun Yamamoto
Translation by M. Kirie Hayashi

A full list of titles appears on Page 236.
Udon Entertainment, 2009-2010
Color, 128-160 pages

For a silly space story, readers should try Yamamoto's short manga series. Her brightly colored retro-style art brings to life the tale of Corona, a girl who thinks that *The Space Patrol* is only a television series — until her classmate recruits her.

143

The Adventures of Tintin series

Story and art by Hergé
Translation by Leslie Lonsdale-Cooper and Michael Turner

Little, Brown, 1945-1976
Color, 64 pages each

Tintin, a young Belgian reporter, often finds himself caught up in a wild assortment of adventures. These include solving strange mysteries, unravelling international political plots, conducting rescue missions, and exploring locales around the world. Aided by his loyal dog, Snowy — and the cynical, grumpy Captain Haddock; the hard-of-hearing but brilliant Professor Calculus; and Thompson and Thomson, two bumbling criminal investigators — Tintin encounters strange scholars, autocratic dictators, and devious spies.

The classic series by Georges Rémi (under the pen name Hergé, as his initials are pronounced in French) features engaging plots and elements from a variety of genres including fantasy, thriller, and science fiction, along with adventure and mystery. Younger readers will enjoy the slapstick humor; older readers will understand the political undertones and cultural commentary. Since the tales are often set in international locales, readers will be introduced to global cultures, even though Hergé often uses imaginary, but familiar, countries as settings. Considering the tales were originally published between the 1930s and the 1970s, today's parents should be aware of controversial content including multiple instances of gun use, references to opium use and drug smuggling, and Captain Haddock's penchant for whiskey. Hergé is often criticized for his use of stereotypes, but throughout the series Tintin is portrayed as a champion of the oppressed. Even with its minor flaws, Tintin is a classic adventure series with clean, expressive art and dense stories with strong appeal. An additional three volumes exist but will have less appeal to young readers: *Tintin in the Congo* (strongly criticized for the book's portrayal of Africans), *Tintin in the Land of the Soviets* (an early work produced while Hergé worked at a right-wing political newspaper), and the unfinished *Tintin and Alph-Art*.

IN THIS SERIES:
A full list of titles appears on page 237.

EDUCATIONAL TIE-INS:
Friendship; World cultures; Gangsters; Al Capone; Native Americans; the Wild West (*Tintin in America*); Egypt; India (*Cigars of the Pharaoh*); China (*The Blue Lotus*); South America; Dictatorship (*The Broken Ear* and *Tintin and the Picaros*); Counterfeiting (*The Black Island*); Monarchy; Politics (*King Ottokar's Sceptre*); Desert; Morocco (*The Crab with the Golden Claws*); Astronomy; Meteorites (*The Shooting Star*); Pirates; Treasure hunt (*Secret of the Unicorn* and *Red Rackham's Treasure*); the Incas; South America (*Seven Crystal Balls* and *Prisoners of the Sun*); the Middle East; Oil (*Land of Black Gold*); Space travel; Astronomy; Spies (*Destination Moon* and *Explorers on the Moon*); Inventions (*The Calculus Affair*); Slavery; Africa (*The Red Sea Sharks*); Rescue; Survival; Tibetan monks; the Abominable Snowman (*Tintin in Tibet*); Television reporters (*The Castafiore Emerald*); Indonesia; Aliens (*Flight 714 to Sydney*)

HEADS UP:
Contains some instances of realistic violence, adult alcohol use, and minor instances of death.

- HERGÉ -
★
THE ADVENTURES OF
TINTIN
★
THE SECRET
OF
THE UNICORN

© Herge/Moulinsart 2011

"WHAT'S NEXT ..."

CITY OF SPIES
Story by Susan Kim and Laurence Klavan
Art by Pascal Dizin

First Second, 2010
Color, 176 pages

Readers who enjoy Tintin's adventures may want to check out this book with a similar clean art style, historical setting, and elements of mystery and adventure. Set in America during World War II, a girl and her new friend uncover a Nazi spy plot.

ALEX RIDER ADVENTURES SERIES
Original stories by Anthony Horowitz
Adapted by Antony Johnston
Art by Kanako and Yuzuru

A full list of titles appears on page 237.
Philomel, 2006-2009
Color, 128-144 pages

Readers looking for an updated take on the adventure story with a strong spy element can check out this trilogy of graphic novels based on the popular Alex Rider prose novels by Anthony Horowitz. Inspired by his late super-spy uncle, 14-year-old Alex Rider chooses a life of perilous adventures, dangerous villains, cool gadgets, and near escapes.

Amelia Earhart: This Broad Ocean

Story by Sarah Stewart Taylor
Art by Ben Towle
Introduction by Eileen Collins

Disney/Hyperion, 2010
Black and white with blue, 80 pages

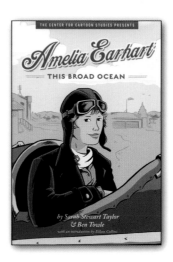

Grace lives in the small Newfoundland town of Trepassey. She dreams of being a reporter and writes her own *Trepassey Herald*, but in 1928 women are expected to stay home, not stick their noses in other people's business. Everything changes, though, when Grace's sleepy fishing village becomes the site of a daring new expedition: Amelia Earhart's attempt to be the first woman to fly across the Atlantic.

Instead of writing a straight biography, Taylor uses Amelia Earhart's story to show readers what life was like for a girl in a small town in the 1920s. Grace's frustration with her circumstances will resonate with young teens who long to grow up. Towle's realistic art is quiet but strong, supporting Taylor's moving story and bringing the village of Trepassey and her inhabitants and visitors to life, from the hardworking fishermen to Amelia's drunken pilot to Grace's cautious snooping. Readers will clearly see the effect that Amelia had on the world and how she left it changed in both large and small ways.

AWARDS:

2011 Young Adult Library Services Association Great Graphic Novel for Teens List; 2011 Amelia Bloomer Project List

EDUCATIONAL TIE-INS:

Amelia Earhart; 1920s; 1930s; Women in history; History of aviation; Exploration; Journalism; Teaching guide available at *http://wildgeeseguides.blogspot.com/2010/01/amelia-earhart-this-broad-ocean.html*; Research notes are included at the end of the book

HEADS UP:

Contains minor use of alcohol by adults.

"WHAT'S NEXT ..."

NO GIRLS ALLOWED: TALES OF DARING WOMEN DRESSED AS MEN FOR LOVE, FREEDOM AND ADVENTURE
Story by Susan Hughes
Art by Willow Dawson

Kids Can Press, 2008
Black and white, 80 pages

Readers who want more stories of strong women throughout history should check out Hughes and Dawson's collection of seven true stories about women who were forced to dress as men to achieve their goals and desires.

THE WRIGHT BROTHERS
Story by Lewis Helfand
Art by Sankha Banerjee

Campfire, 2011
Color, 72 pages

Budding aeronautics buffs will want to read this engaging, thorough biography of the brothers who developed the airplane. Helfand and Banerjee highlight important and lesser-known details — such as the effect the Wright brothers' engineering-minded mother had on them and the struggles they faced long after flying for the first time, trying to keep credit for their work.

Amulet series

Story and art by Kazu Kibuishi
Colors by Jason Caffoe

Scholastic/Graphix, 2008-2011
Color, 192-224 pages

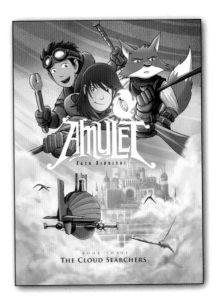

After the death of their father, Emily, Navin, and their mother move into an old house belonging to their great-grandfather, who mysteriously vanished years ago. Just after Emily discovers a strange amulet, her mother is kidnapped. The siblings descend into an underground world, where they discover that their great-grandfather was part of a group of guardians with magical powers and that those powers have been passed to Emily. With the help of new friends, the two children rescue their mother and decide against returning home in order for Emily to fulfill her destiny and save the land from the evil Elf King. Emily, with her family and protectors, travels across Alledia meeting new allies, making new enemies, and searching for answers on how to defeat the Elf King — while trying to control the growing and uncontrollable powers of the amulet.

Readers hungry for an adventure story with elements of fantasy and science fiction will devour Kibuishi's epic series. Kibuishi introduces readers to a wide range of characters in addition to the main protagonists, from the heroic Leon Redbeard to the adorable Misket to the deadly Elf King. *Amulet* is a dark, dramatic series with many high-stakes moments, but at its core it is about the importance of family and friends and growing up. Kibuishi's art skillfully depicts the landscapes of Alledia but is also successful in illustrating action sequences and emotional character moments.

IN THIS SERIES:

Book One: The Stonekeeper
Book Two: The Stonekeeper's Curse
Book Three: The Cloud Searchers
Book Four: The Last Council

EDUCATIONAL TIE-INS:

Friendship; Family; Quest stories; Responsibility

HEADS UP:

Contains some instances of realistic violence, mature themes, and death.

"WHAT'S NEXT ..."

GHOSTOPOLIS
Story and art by Doug TenNapel

Scholastic/Graphix, 2010
Color, 272 pages

Readers who enjoyed the otherworldly setting and the quest elements of *Amulet* might want to check out this graphic novel about a boy who finds himself in the spirit world pursued by an evil ruler who wants the boy's special abilities in order to gain unstoppable power. Lighter in tone and far less epic, *Ghostopolis* shares the same imaginative spirit and determined protagonist found in Kibuishi's series.

Archie: Freshman Year series

Story by Batton Lash
Art by Bill Galvan and Bob Smith

Archie Comics, 2009-2011
Color, 112 pages and 128 pages

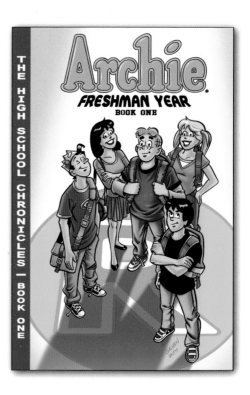

As Archie and his friends prepare for their first day at Riverdale High, they discover that their good friend Jughead won't be joining them, since his family is moving away. Without his best friend, Archie starts high school on the wrong foot, closely watched by new principal Mr. Weatherbee, and soon makes enemies with the school's bully, Jared McGerk. While dealing with new teachers and trying to keep up with his studies, Archie enjoys the company of his friends — especially Betty and Veronica — and makes new friends, including Pencilneck G, a laid-back skateboarder; Chuck Clayton, an aspiring comic-book artist; and Dilton Doiley, Riverdale's science genius.

Combining the innocent spirit of *Archie* comics with current cultural references and a racially diverse cast, Lash gives *Archie* an update and takes readers to the beginnings of the Riverdale gang's high-school career. Readers will find all the typical *Archie* elements in this series, including humor, friendships, and high-school crushes, with little edgy content. Perfect for middle-schoolers, this series may ease the anxiety of transitioning to high school but mainly is light, fun reading.

IN THIS SERIES:
Book One: The High School Chronicles
Book Two: The Missing Chapters

EDUCATIONAL TIE-INS:

School; Teachers; Bullying; Peer pressure; Friendship

"WHAT'S NEXT ..."

ITAZURA NA KISS SERIES
Story and art by Kaoru Tada

A full list of titles appears on page 238.

Digital Manga Publishing, 2009-2011
Black and white, 300-376 pages

Readers who like the high-school high jinks of *Archie* but who want a slightly more mature story will enjoy the romance and humor of Tada's classic manga series, which takes Kotoko from an awkward high-school student, through college, and into a happy marriage.

The Arrival

Story and art by Shaun Tan

Scholastic/Arthur Levine Books, 2006
Black and white with sepia, 128 pages

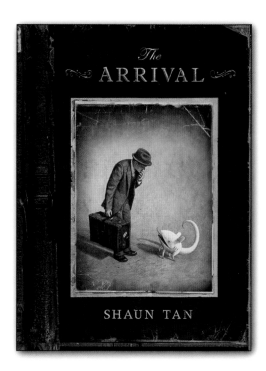

A man leaves his wife and child behind in a dangerous land and travels to a strange new country, where he meets other immigrants, learns new customs, and gradually adapts to a life of freedom.

Tan's wordless graphic novel uses soft pencil work on sepia-toned pages to tell an allegorical story about the immigrant's journey. The world the nameless man immigrates to may seem like a fantasyland, but the fantastical images are meant to show the reader how strange, unsettling, and confusing life is in a new country. Readers discover the past of the man and each of the immigrants he meets in flashbacks that hint at communist Eastern Europe, the Chinese Cultural Revolution, World War II, and World War I. Even though *The Arrival* is wordless, readers need some knowledge of the American immigrant experience in order to understand Tan's moving, highly detailed art.

AWARDS:

2007 New South Wales Premier's Literary Award for Book of the Year; 2008 Young Adult Library Services Association Great Graphic Novel for Teens List — Top Ten; 2008 Young Adult Library Services Association Best Books for Young Adults List — Top Ten; 2008 Association for Library Service to Children Notable Children's Book; 2008 Boston Globe-Horn Book Award Special Citation for Excellence in Graphic Storytelling

EDUCATIONAL TIE-INS:

American immigration, early 20th century; Allegory; Teacher's book notes available at *http://www.scool.scholastic.com.au/schoolzone/toolkit/The_Arrival.pdf*; Teaching resources available at *http://www2.scholastic.com/browse/collection.jsp?id=153*

"WHAT'S NEXT ..."

AROUND THE WORLD: THREE REMARKABLE JOURNEYS
Story and art by Matt Phelan

Candlewick, 2011
Color, 240 pages

Unlike Tan's exploration of the forced immigrant experience, Phelan's nonfiction anthology tells the story of three people who each chose to circumnavigate the globe during the 19th century. Phelan's quiet storytelling and softly colored pencil work make this book a good companion to Tan's fictional tale, especially for readers interested in the reasons people decide to travel from one country to another.

© Text and illustration copyright 2006 Shaun Tan

Astronaut Academy: Zero Gravity

Story and art by Dave Roman

First Second, 2011
Black and white, 192 pages

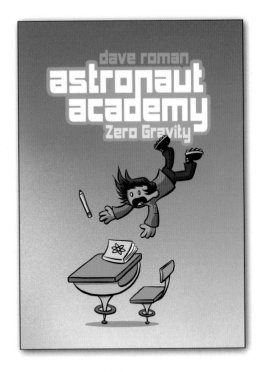

As the newest student at the esteemed Astronaut Academy, Hakata Soy tries his best to blend in despite his past as the leader of a transforming robot-vehicle super-team. While adjusting to life at his new school, Hakata is introduced to strange teachers and even stranger students. One of the students recognizes Hakata because his team saved her people from an evil race called The Gotcha Birds. In revenge, The Gotcha Birds steal Hakata's robot doppelgänger and reprogram him to infiltrate the school and destroy him.

Roman's tongue-in-cheek science-fiction school story features a huge cast of quirky characters that readers will either laugh at or identify with, including the spoiled rich girl Maribelle Melonbelly, the sports-obsessed Tak, and Spike, the boy who is fond of other boys. This book will appeal to fans of video games and Japanese cartoons with its overly dramatic, self-aware dialogue and hidden pop-culture references. Most of the humor in Roman's story lies in the way this book makes the familiar teachers, classes, and extracurricular activities of school seem random and silly. Roman's bold art skilfully conveys both the expanse of space and the narrowness of the classrooms where detailed interactions between characters take place.

EDUCATIONAL TIE-INS:

Teachers; Space; Friendship; Relationships; Bravery

HEADS UP:

Contains minor instances of realistic violence and very minor kissing.

"WHAT'S NEXT …"

HOLLOW FIELDS OMNIBUS
Story and art by Madeleine Rosca

Seven Seas, 2009
Black and white, 544 pages

Unexpectedly landing at Miss Weaver's Academy for the Scientifically Gifted and Ethically Unfettered, Lucy Snow must prove that she can handle the coursework before she joins the other students with low grades in a detention from which they never return. Rosca's story is part steampunk, part Harry Potter, but will appeal to *Astronaut Academy* fans who like stories about strange schools and quirky characters.

Bad Island

Story and art by Doug TenNapel
Colors by Katherine Garner and Josh Kenfield

Scholastic/Graphix, 2011
Color, 224 pages

Reluctantly, teenage Reese accompanies his parents and sister on a family boating vacation. When a violent storm hits, the family is shipwrecked on a mysterious island filled with unrecognizable plants and bizarre animals. After stumbling upon an alien artifact, Reese's parents are captured by spear-wielding creatures, leaving Reese and his sister to save them and find a way off the island. Fighting off increasingly dangerous otherworldly creatures, Reese and his family realize that they're caught in the middle of a centuries-old conflict between two alien races and that the island is more than it appears.

TenNapel's highly imaginative adventure has a rich backstory with unusually designed aliens that will appeal to science-fiction fans. Even non-SF readers will laugh at the humorous, yet realistic, portrayal of Reese's family with all its members' squabbles but also their strong love for one another. The story is fast-paced and action-packed but includes violent scenes, as family members defend themselves against dangerous creatures: Reese shoots one with a flare gun, and his mother stabs one with a spear. TenNapel uses silhouetted panels to lessen the graphic impact in many of these scenes.

EDUCATIONAL TIE-INS:

Family; Survival; Aliens

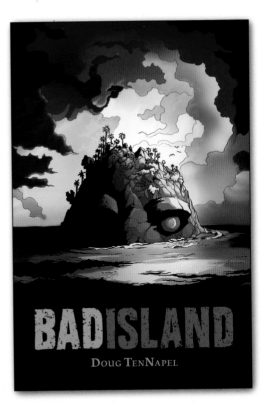

HEADS UP:

Contains some instances of realistic violence and death.

"WHAT'S NEXT ..."

INTO THE VOLCANO
Story and art by Don Wood

Scholastic/Blue Sky Press, 2008
Color, 176 pages

Readers looking for a more realistic island survival story can check out this graphic novel about a pair of brothers, Duffy and Sumo, who face a volcano. Even though the story of these two brothers is more true-to-life than that of Reese and his family, the theme of courage and family togetherness is important in both books.

From *Bad Island* by Doug TenNapel. Scholastic Inc./Graphix. © 2011 by Doug TenNapel. Used by permission.

Bone series

Story and art by Jeff Smith
Colors by Steve Hamaker

Scholastic/Graphix, 2005-2009
Color, 118-214 pages

Three cousins — Fone Bone, Phoney
Bone, and Smiley Bone — are run out
of their homeland when one of Phoney's
schemes goes awry. After wandering through
a desert, they lose each other in a strange
valley. Thorn, a beautiful girl, and her tough-
as-nails Gran'ma Ben rescue Fone Bone and
help him find his cousins, but he doesn't
realize that his new friends are far more than
they appear to be. As Fone Bone learns more
about his rescuers, he becomes enmeshed in a
dark secret, is chased by an ancient evil, and
finds himself honor bound to help a princess
in disguise, an enigmatic dragon, and all of
the creatures — human and animal — who
live in The Valley.

Bone is the perfect example of a classic
comics series for *all* ages, accessible to
readers as young as second or third grade, but
with layered nuances that older readers will
appreciate. Starting off with light humor and
action, this series gradually builds to more
serious fantasy adventure. Smith contrasts the
small but sturdy Bone cousins — who look
like Casper the Friendly Ghost, but with legs
— and the stupid but dangerous Rat Creatures
with the more realistic and more deadly
humans, creating an epic story with long-
lasting appeal. The companion volumes offer
further tales set in the *Bone* universe, both
before and after the original series.

IN THIS SERIES:

A full list of titles appears on page 239.

AWARDS:

1993, 1994, and 1995 Will Eisner Comic
Industry Award for Best Humor Publication;
1994 Will Eisner Comic Industry Awards
for Best Serialized Story; 1994 and 1995
Will Eisner Comic Industry Awards for Best

Continuing Series; 1994, 1995, and 1998 Will
Eisner Comic Industry Awards for Best Writer/
Artist; 2002 Will Eisner Comic Industry Award for
Best Painter (Charles Vess for *Rose*); 2005 Will
Eisner Comic Industry Award for Best Graphic
Album; 1994-1997, 1999, 2000, 2003, and 2005
Harvey Award for Best Cartoonist (Writer/Artist);
1994 and 2005 Harvey Award for Best Graphic
Album of Previously Published Work; 1994
Harvey Award for Special Award for Humor; 2002
Young Adult Library Services Association Popular
Paperbacks: Graphic Novels List

EDUCATIONAL TIE-INS:
Responsibility/Duty; Friendship; Family

HEADS UP:
Contains minor use of alcohol by adults, multiple
instances of realistic and cartoon violence,
several deaths, strong or frightening scenes, and
some name-calling.

"WHAT'S NEXT ..."

THE WIZARD'S TALE
Story by Kurt Busiek
Art by David Wenzel

IDW, 2010
Color, 144 pages

Busiek and Wenzel's tale of the old wizard Bafflerog
Rumplewhisker, who must decide between doing
something evil (as expected) or something good
(which will change his world forever), is a good
choice for *Bone* fans who loved the high fantasy and
hard choices of Smith's epic series.

Brain Camp

Story by Susan Kim and Laurence Klavan

Art by Faith Erin Hicks

Colors by Hilary Sycamore

First Second, 2010
Color, 160 pages

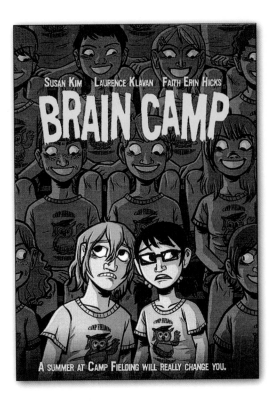

When Jenna (an aimless dreamer) and Lucas (a slacker delinquent) are offered spots in an exclusive educational camp, their parents jump at the chance. Both teens arrive to find typical camping unpleasantries, but also strange bird fetuses and campers who go from relatively normal to super-intelligent zombies overnight. The camp director convinces Jenna and Lucas that the camp suffers from a disease, and they reluctantly agree to be vaccinated and deal with the "temporary" side effects. Soon after, they discover the camp's dark secret and must find a way to save their fellow campers before turning into obedient zombies themselves.

Horror for middle-grade readers is rare, but this is a good example of the genre with its gruesome imagery, suspense, and a sense of desperation that fans will love. There's more than scares and gross-outs; the book also explores preteen issues including the pressures of achieving, parental expectations, and the fear of losing one's individuality. Sex often goes hand-in-hand with the horror genre, but here it is tame — with the two main characters exchanging a few kisses and one subtly drawn scene in which Lucas wakes to discover he has had a wet dream.

EDUCATIONAL TIE-INS:

Summer camp; Self-esteem; Identity; Parents

HEADS UP:

Contains some realistic violence, strong or frightening scenes, kissing, death, and explores issues related to adolescent puberty.

"WHAT'S NEXT ..."

GOOSEBUMPS SERIES

Story and art by various

CREEPY CREATURES
TERROR TRIPS
SCARY SUMMER

Scholastic/Graphix, 2006-2007
Black and white, 144 pages each

Readers looking for more suspenseful and creepy tales should look to the master of young-readers horror, R.L. Stine, with this trio of graphic anthologies that adapt some of his most popular stories.

ROMANCE

Chiggers

Story and art by Hope Larson

Simon & Schuster/Aladdin Mix, 2008
Black and white, 176 pages

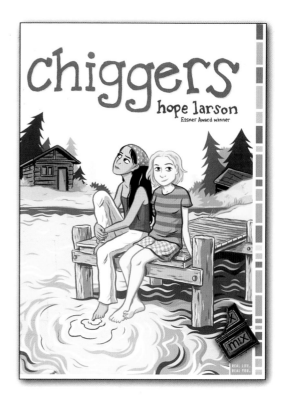

Abby returns to summer camp as the same geeky girl, only to find that her friends have all changed: Rose is now a cabin assistant and has little time for her; Beth has piercings, is music-obsessed, and seems too cool; and her other cabin mates just don't want to be there. When Shasta arrives, Abby feels less like an outsider but senses something strange about her new friend. Shasta introduces Abby to Teal, a *Dungeons & Dragons* fan who calls Abby an elf. She spends the summer trying to get his attention while navigating the ups and downs of her old and new friendships.

Larson captures the intensity of friendships of this age group with its chaotic mix of emotions moving quickly from jealousy and pettiness to sweetness and warmth. Girls will relate to late-bloomer Abby's feelings of being an outsider, as well as her search for identity. Larson's art contains an appealing dreamy quality packed with interesting visual details. The romantic element of the story is tame and culminates with an innocent kiss. Larson occasionally uses strong language (including such words as "loser," "bitch," and "jerk") to express the characters' volatile relationships.

EDUCATIONAL TIE-INS:

Camp; Friendship; Identity

HEADS UP:

Contains minor name-calling and some kissing and explores issues related to adolescent puberty.

"WHAT'S NEXT ..."

WAR AT ELLSMERE

Story and art by Faith Erin Hicks

SLG Publishing, 2008
Color, 156 pages

Even with this book's unexpected fantasy twist at the end, readers who liked *Chiggers'* realistic handling of young teen girl issues will enjoy reading about Jun, the new girl in a posh boarding school who faces snobby bullies.

Clan Apis

Story and art by Jay Hosler, Ph.D.

Active Synapse, 2000
Black and white, 160 pages

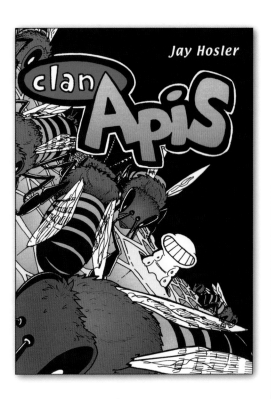

Nyuki is the newest member of Clan Apis — and possibly the most fearful. The young bee survives one trip outside the hive but, after almost being eaten by a praying mantis, attacked by a crab spider, and then rolled over by a dung beetle's ball of dung, she has no interest in venturing outside ever again. Her sister Dvorah steps in to show her the most important rules of life: No one survives it, and life should be lived to the fullest.

Bee-scientist Hosler's graphic novel is partly about the life cycle of a honeybee and partly about the importance of taking chances. Readers will learn about the small insects that give us honey and wax and that pollinate flowers in the course of reading an unexpectedly moving story of life, death, and friendship. The art consists of realistic drawings that use the minimum amount of cartooning needed to convey human emotions using insect bodies. Even though the story is serious and the characters face real dangers, there is a heart-warming sense of inter-connectedness that will leave readers touched and eager to learn more about bees, other insects, and their roles in the world.

AWARDS:

1998 Xeric Award Winner

EDUCATIONAL TIE-INS:

Life-cycle; Science; Bees and other insects; Scientists

HEADS UP:

Contains some realistic violence and death of the main character.

"WHAT'S NEXT ..."

LEO GEO AND HIS MIRACULOUS JOURNEY THROUGH THE CENTER OF THE EARTH
Story and art by Jon Chad

Roaring Brook Press, 2012
Black and white, 40 pages

Readers who love the science meets fiction aspect of *Clan Apis* but who want a bit more adventure will enjoy Leo's story. Using a variety of implements — from a drill to his own hands and feet — Leo burrows toward the center of the Earth and out the other side, encountering strange creatures along the way. Chad's unusual blend of fiction and fact is exciting, and readers will love that, to read it, they have to hold the book vertically, flipping it over midway through the story.

© 2011 Jay Hosler

Courtney Crumrin series

Story and art by Ted Naifeh
Color by Warren Wucinich

Oni Press, 2012 (reissue)
Color, 128-144 pages

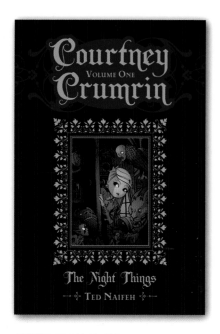

Courtney and her money-grubbing parents move in with their rich uncle Aloysius, supposedly to take care of him — but her parents want to take advantage of his large house in a trendy suburb. Quickly realizing there is something odd about her new home, Courtney discovers that she has unexpected powers, which come in handy when dealing with the mundane bullies at school, the fairies who kidnap human children for a slave market, and the haughty and misguided members of the witches' coven she is expected to join. Uncle Aloysius proves to be an unexpected mentor, but his own secrets keep him from showing affection to anyone, even his talented grandniece.

Naifeh's dark series is edgy, but still middle-school-appropriate. Readers will understand Courtney's disappointment with her shallow parents, her feelings of alienation, her longing for love, her desire for power, and her fear of misusing that power. Courtney is smart but she sometimes allows those smarts to get the better of her (and learns resultant painful lessons). Naifeh's moody art perfectly captures the dark paranormal feel of his story. He doesn't shy away from death and violence, though the majority of it is off-page, and there is some mild but possibly offensive language, such as "ass" and "bugger."

IN THIS SERIES:

A full list of titles appears on page 241.

EDUCATIONAL TIE-INS:

Duty; Responsibility; Bullies; Abuse of power; Family; Folklore

HEADS UP:

Contains multiple instances of realistic violence, death, strong language, strong or frightening scenes, and some name-calling.

"WHAT'S NEXT ..."

GUNNERKRIGG COURT SERIES
Story and art by Thomas Siddell

A full list of titles appears on page 241.
Archaia Studios Press, 2008-2011
Color, 280-296 pages

Between the haunted wood and the Minotaur in the basement and the demon who takes over her stuffed toy, Antimony's beginning to suspect there's something a little strange about her school, Gunnerkrigg Court: something in which her dead mother and missing father might have been involved. *Courtney Crumrin* fans who like dark fantasy will want to check out the print editions of Siddell's popular webcomic.

Crogan's Adventures series

Story and art by Chris Schweizer

Oni Press, 2008-2012
Black and white, 176-212 pages

Dr. Crogan has his own way of helping his sons resolve problems: He tells them tales of their Crogan ancestors, each of whom faced hardships at different times in history. First, there is "Catfish" Crogan who is forced to turn pirate in the early 1700s and must help save a town from a ruthless fellow pirate. Then, there is Peter Crogan, a Legionnaire serving in North Africa in 1912, who is trapped between duty to a clueless commanding officer and his own sense of right and wrong. And finally, the brothers William and Charles Crogan find themselves on opposite sides of the Revolutionary War.

Schweizer takes deep historical issues and turns them into thrilling action tales. All of the Crogan books can be read without much knowledge of the history of the different time periods, but readers will come away from the books wanting to know more about that history. The books offer much for discussion groups or classes to talk about, while remaining exciting stories. Because of the topics covered, there is violence, but Schweizer's cartoonish art keeps the disturbing aspects as much off-page as possible — and his creative use of historical language keeps swearing to a minimum, despite the settings. The breathless pace of the stories and the strong male role models make these excellent choices for boys.

IN THIS SERIES:

A full list of titles appears on page 242.

AWARDS:

2010 Young Adult Library Services Association Great Graphic Novel for Teens List (*Crogan's Vengeance*)

EDUCATIONAL TIE-INS:

Family trees/genealogy; Pirates (*Crogan's Vengeance*); Early 18th century (*Crogan's Vengeance*); French Colonial Empire in Africa (*Crogan's March*); French Foreign Legion (*Crogan's March*); Army of Africa (*Crogan's March*); Africa, 1912 (*Crogan's March*); Colonialism (*Crogan's March*); Revolutionary War (*Crogan's Loyalty*); American colonies (*Crogan's Loyalty*)

HEADS UP:

Contains minor use of alcohol by adults, multiple instances of realistic violence, death of the main character, strong language (though the words used are historical), and some name-calling.

"WHAT'S NEXT ..."

DESTINY'S HAND:
ULTIMATE PIRATE COLLECTION
Story by Nunzio DeFilippis and Christina Weir
Art by Melvin Calingo

Seven Seas, 2009
Black and white, 496 pages

Readers looking for pirate adventures will enjoy *Destiny's Hand*, the story of a runway girl who decides to become a pirate — and the ship that cannot be sunk. This collection features more fantasy elements than the *Crogan's Adventure* series — as well as more violence — but the themes of honor and loyalty remain the same.

ROMANCE • SCHOOL & FAMILY • SPORTS & GAMES

Cross Game series

Story and art by Mitsuru Adachi
Translation by Ralph Yamada (Volume 1)
and Lillian Olsen (Volumes 1-8)

Viz, 2010-2012
Black and white, 376-576 pages

Ko's family runs a sporting-goods shop near the Tsukishima family's batting cages and coffee shop. Ko and the four Tsukishima sisters have grown up together, and he is especially close to the second daughter, Wakaba, who is his age. When tragedy strikes in fifth grade and later, when Ko and third daughter, Aoba, move into high school, they find solace in their shared love of baseball. The changes of adolescence, however, force them to think about their often argumentative friendship and whether it might be something deeper.

Adachi's series is perfect for readers who want baseball action tempered with touching emotions and a bit of romance. Even with Adachi's rounded, cartoonish art, the characters seem realistic, with distinct personalities, and boy readers in particular will identify with either the laid-back Ko or one of his teammates. There are drawings of girls in their underwear or skimpy bathing suits in every volume — not surprising in a series aimed at middle-school boys — but the female characters are not just eye-candy. Aoba, in particular, is a strong young woman, and the other female characters are just as smart and resourceful. Often covering over half of each oversized volume, the baseball games give sports fans a lot to enjoy, but readers who like gentle, realistic romances will enjoy the books, as well.

IN THIS SERIES:
A full list of titles appears on page 242.

AWARDS:
2009 54th Annual Shogakukan Manga Award for shonen (boys') manga; 2011 Young Adult Library Services Association Great Graphic Novel for Teens List (*Volume 1*)

EDUCATIONAL TIE-INS:
Teamwork; Dedication; Loss of a sibling; Loss of a friend

HEADS UP:
Contains some cartoon violence, death, kissing, and minor instances of characters wearing suggestive clothing. Story reads right-to-left.

"WHAT'S NEXT ..."

PRINCE OF TENNIS **SERIES**
Story and art by Takeshi Konomi
Translation by Joe Yamazaki
A full list of titles appears on page 242.

Viz, 2004-2011
Black and white, 176-208 pages

For a story with a little more focus on teamwork and sports and a little less romance and fewer skimpy outfits, readers should try *Prince of Tennis*. Ryoma, a 12-year-old tennis prodigy, begins competing against players a few years older and learns that being best may not be enough to gain the respect of his teammates.

Cross Game © 2005 Mitsuru Adachi/Shogakukan

Hereville: How Mirka Got Her Sword

Story and art by Barry Deutsch

Abrams/Amulet, 2010
Color, 144 pages

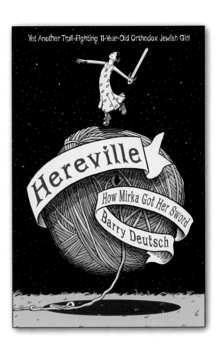

Yet Another Troll-Fighting 11-Year-Old Orthodox Jewish Girl

Hereville

How Mirka Got Her Sword

Barry Deutsch

Living in an Orthodox Jewish family, 11-year-old Mirka is encouraged to get involved with tasks that are appropriate for a woman to do, such as knitting. But Mirka's dream is to fight dragons, and she tests her courage and strength defending her little brother Zindel from bullies. When Mirka discovers the home of a witch, she is harassed by a giant pig, which she later rescues from the same bullies who threatened her brother. For saving her pig, the witch offers Mirka a reward: instructions on how to acquire a sword so she can be a true dragon-slayer — but only if she can defeat a troll first.

Deutsch's story incorporates information about the Orthodox Jewish culture — including religious celebrations, customs, and language — seamlessly without alienating non-Jewish readers. All readers will relate to Mirka's struggle to find her place in her community and her quest for identity. Her rejection of traditional roles and her rebellious nature ring true, and the discovery that her strength is found in her cultural background may surprise young readers. Deutch's art is packed with comedy and action and possesses a strong sense of storytelling. His panel layouts are clear but far from boring: packed with subtle details that add to the charm of the characters and the interest of the story.

AWARDS:

2011 Young Adult Library Services Association Great Graphic Novel for Teens List; 2011 Association of Jewish Libraries Sydney Taylor Award Winner for Older Readers

EDUCATIONAL TIE-INS:

Family; Jewish celebrations & customs; Jewish folklore; Identity; Bullying

HEADS UP:

Contains minor instances of realistic violence.

"WHAT'S NEXT ..."

FOILED
Story by Jane Yolen
Art by Mike Cavallaro

First Second, 2010
Color, 160 pages

With her only interests being fencing and role-playing games, plain, color-blind Aliera has trouble fitting in — but a new boy in school turns out to be something completely unexpected. Like *Hereville*, the slightly more mature *Foiled* also blends fantasy with the real world and offers readers another heroine who knows the importance of a good sword and the strength to wield it.

Cover illustrations © 2010 Barry Deutsch and Interior illustrations © 2010 Barry Deutsch

Hikaru no Go series

Story by Yumi Hotta
Art by Takeshi Obata
Supervised by Yukari Umezawa
Translation by Andy Nakatani (volumes 1-12); Naoko Amemiya (volumes 13-23)
English script supervised by Janice Kim

Viz, 2004-2011
Black and white, 192-216 pages

Hikaru Shindo, a middle-school student with no particular interests, stumbles across a haunted Go board and unwittingly finds himself bound to Fujiwara-no-Sai, the ghost of a Go master from the 1500s who died in disgrace. Sai convinces Hikaru to let him play Go using Hikaru's body, but, once Hikaru gets a taste for the game, he decides that he wants to learn to play himself. Hikaru learns the intricacies of the game, makes new friends, and finds an unexpected shot at a career as a pro Go player.

Hotta and Obata take an idea that shouldn't work — 23 volumes about a boy playing an ancient Asian board game — and turn it into a gripping and moving tale of friendship, rivalry, and commitment. Readers do not need to know anything about Go to enjoy Hikaru's journey from novice to pro. As the story progresses, readers learn the basics of the game and become riveted by the depth that Hotta brings to each character. Obata's skillful art is extremely realistic, but he adds plenty of movement lines and other elements from action comics to keep the story moving quickly along. The adults in the story drink and smoke, but the teens are too focused on their studies to do more than argue and swear eternal rivalry with one another. Readers who love sharp characters and a compelling story with a hint of fantasy will love this series.

IN THIS SERIES:
A full list of titles appears on page 244.

AWARDS:
1999 45th Annual Shogakukan Manga Award for shonen (boys'); 2003 Tezuka Osamu Cultural Prize — Creative Award; 2009 Young Adult Library Services Association Great Graphic Novel for Teens List (volumes 12 and 13)

EDUCATIONAL TIE-INS:
Commitment; Hard work; Friendship; Hero's journey; American Go Foundation school programs: *http://agfgo.org/schools.html*; American Go Foundation library programs: *http://agfgo. org/library.htm*; Tiger's Mouth (American Go Foundation's site for kids): *http://tigersmouth.org*

HEADS UP:
Contains minor instances of alcohol use and cigarette smoking by adults. Story reads right-to-left.

"WHAT'S NEXT ..."

BAKÉGYAMON SERIES
Story and art by Mitsuhisa Tamura
Original concept by Kazuhiro Fujita
Translation by Labaaman, HC Language Solutions, Inc.

A full list of titles appears on page 244.
Viz, 2009
Black and white, 200-216 pages

Readers who enjoy the heavy gaming and slight paranormal elements of *Hikaru No Go* may enjoy this equally game-focused manga series. Sanshiro craves adventure and gets his wish when he is sent to Backwards Japan to play in a series of challenging games with the help of creatures and monsters that he can summon from cards found on his adventures.

Hikaru-No Go © 1998 by Yumi Hotta, Takeshi Obata/Shueisha Inc.

Kid Beowulf series

Story and art by Alexis E. Fajardo

Bowler Hat Comics, 2008-2010
Black and white, 192-244 pages

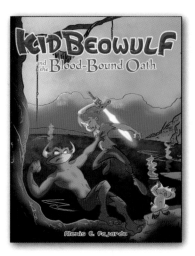

When a hot-headed young prince named Hrothgar makes a deal with a dragon, events are set in motion that lead to the birth of twins: a boy named Beowulf and a dragon-human hybrid named Grendel. But Hrothgar's past mistakes come back to haunt him, and Beowulf and Grendel are exiled from Daneland. Traveling to Francia to see their uncle Ogier, who left years before in protest of Hrothgar's harsh ways, Beowulf and Grendel find themselves caught between the ailing King Charlemagne and the traitorous Ganelon, who has Charlemagne's nephew, Roland, under his control. The brothers must work with the banished peers of the realm to save Charlemagne before King Marsilion invades from Hispania.

Fajardo combines ancient epic poetry — the Anglo-Saxon poem *Beowulf*, the French poem *The Song of Roland*, and the Italian poem *Orlando Furioso* — with modern anachronisms to create a part-fantasy, part-history romp that will appeal to readers who like adventure. Readers won't require knowledge of these poems to enjoy Fajardo's series, though each book opens with a character guide and an overview of the traditional story. These broadly adapted retellings add a lot of fun and fighting to the basic bones of the classic tales. The length of the books, the large number of characters, and the small type make this series ideal for stronger readers and those looking for historical action.

IN THIS SERIES:

Kid Beowulf and the Blood-Bound Oath
Kid Beowulf and the Song of Roland

EDUCATIONAL TIE-INS:

Beowulf; 8th century Europe; Heroism; Destiny; The Song of Roland; Orlando Furioso (*The Song of Roland*)

HEADS UP:

Contains some realistic and cartoon violence and death.

"WHAT'S NEXT …"

BEOWULF
Story by Stephan Petrucha
Art by Kody Chamberlain

HarperCollins, 2007
Color, 96 pages

Readers looking for a middle-school-appropriate graphic-novel version of the original *Beowulf*, rather than *Kid Beowulf*'s looser retelling, should look for Petrucha's strong abridgement.

USAGI YOJIMBO SERIES
Story and art by Stan Sakai

A full list of titles appears on page 245.
Fantagraphics (books 1-7), Dark Horse (books 8+), 1987-2011
Black and white, 64-244 pages

Older readers looking for more historical-fantasy adventure should give Stan Sakai's epic series a try. Miyamoto Usagi, a rabbit samurai (loosely based on real-life samurai Miyamoto Musashi), travels a 17th century Japan populated by animals, offering his services as a bodyguard.

Lila and Ecco's Do It Yourself Comics Club

Story and art by Willow Dawson

Kids Can Press, 2010
Black and white, 112 pages

Best friends Lila and Ecco head to the local comic-book convention dressed as their favorite characters and attend a workshop on making comics. A panel of comic-book creators discusses the wide range of comics that can be produced. Inspired by their role models, Lila and Ecco get to work following the steps outlined by the panel of creators. The two brainstorm ideas; write a script; pencil, ink, and letter their work; create a cover; photocopy; and bind their comics — and, finally, share them with their friends.

Dawson's story about two friends making their own comics shows kids that they can easily create, publish, and share their own stories. All the important basics of making comics are covered in this book, but it also includes a strong focus on such initial stages of creation as brainstorming, outlining, and research, as well as the importance of revising and editing. Each chapter presents a new lesson and builds on the last, culminating in the final published comic book. The different ways that Lila and Ecco approach their work will encourage readers to be flexible when creating their own stories. Packed with great tips on writing interesting scripts, believable characters, and page-turning comics-page layouts, this book is ideal for aspiring comics creators.

EDUCATIONAL TIE-INS:

Creative writing; Art and artists

"WHAT'S NEXT ..."

MAKING COMICS
Story and art by Scott McCloud

HarperCollins, 2006
Black and white, 272 pages

Older readers ready for more advanced guidance on making their own comics should look at McCloud's third book in his comics-creation trilogy. Much as readers learned the process of creating comics through Dawson's two characters, a cartoon version of Scott McCloud addresses readers with tips and advice on how to make drawings become a story. Be aware, however, that McCloud is writing for adults, and it is advisable to look at his vocabulary and panel examples to evaluate the volume's use with a specific child.

Material from *Lila and Ecco's Do-It-Yourself Comics Club* is used by permission of Kids Can Press Ltd., Toronto.
Text & illustrations © 2010 Willow Dawson.

Mouse Guard series

Story and art by David Petersen

Archaia Studios Press, 2007-2009
Color, 200 pages each

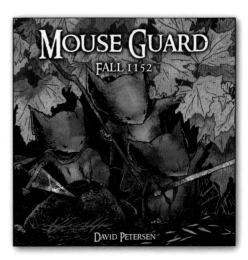

Members of the Mouse Guard are the protectors of all mice, guarding the pathways between the mouse settlements and allowing the safe passage of tradesmice, leaders, and others. But a traitor in their midst plans to overthrow the Guard and bring all mouse towns under one leader. The loyal members of the Guard must find the traitor, save the town of Lockhaven, and ensure that the mice there can survive the winter.

Readers who love fantasy that combines a medieval-like setting with political intrigue and the threat of war — as in Brian Jacques' *Redwall* books — will thrill at Petersen's epic series. He gives readers a fully realized world in which mice face danger with swords and courage. The highly detailed art clearly shows the small stature of his heroes while making their world feel both old-fashioned and realistic. There is no magic in this story, other than that of good storytelling, but there's much fighting, though it is never too graphic or bloody for a middle-school audience. In the companion volume, *Legends of the Guard*, Petersen allows other comics artists to tell tales set in the world of *Mouse Guard*.

IN THIS SERIES:

Fall 1152
Winter 1152
Legends of the Guard, Vol. 1

Stories and art by Jeremy Bastian, Ted Naifeh, Alex Sheikman, Sean Rubin, Alex Kain, Terry Moore, Lowell Francis, Katie Cook, Guy Davis, Nate Pride, Jason Shawn Alexander, Craig Rousseau, Karl Kerschl, Mark Smylie, João Lemos, and David Petersen

Archaia Studios Press, 2010
Color, 144 pages

AWARDS:

2008 Will Eisner Comic Industry Award for Best Publication for Kids and Best Graphic Album — Reprint; 2008 Young Adult Library Services Association Great Graphic Novel for Teens List

EDUCATIONAL TIE-INS:

Folklore; Responsibility

HEADS UP:

Contains minor use of alcohol by adult characters, multiple instances of realistic violence, and death.

"WHAT'S NEXT ..."

THE HOBBIT: AN ILLUSTRATED EDITION OF THE FANTASY CLASSIC

Story by J.R.R. Tolkien
Adapted by Charles Dixon with Sean Deming
Art by David Wenzel

Del Rey, 2001
Color, 144 pages

Tolkien is the reigning king of high fantasy, and readers who love the deep, layered quality of Petersen's series will enjoy this adaptation of the story of Bilbo, a simple Hobbit, who finds himself on a journey with a pack of dwarfs and an enigmatic wizard named Gandalf.

My Boyfriend Is a Monster series

Story and art by Various

Lerner/Graphic Universe, 2010-2012
Black and white (Vols. 1-3), black and white with color (Vol. 4), 128 pages each

High-school romance is tricky enough, when it's between a jock and a nerd or an orchestra geek and the new guy in school. When these girls discover that their new boyfriends are really a fairy prince, a ghost, Frankenstein's monster, possibly a vampire, or infected with a zombie plague, *that's* when they step up and fight to be with the one they love, despite their boyfriends' supernatural backgrounds.

Each volume in this series features a different author, a different artist, and a different monster boyfriend; each shares light touches of humor, against-the-odds romance, and a supply of girl power. Observant readers will spot the two characters that connect all the books in the series, but the paranormal romance is the component that will keep their interest in each subsequent volume. Relationships are tame enough for middle-schoolers, but the manga-sized volumes, bold black and white art, and likeable main characters make these a hit for young high-schoolers, as well.

IN THIS SERIES:

#1: *I Love Him to Pieces*
Story by Evonne Tsang; art by Janina Görrissen

#2: *Made for Each Other*
Story by Paul D. Storrie; art by Eldon Cowgur

#3: *My Boyfriend Bites*
Story by Dan Jolley; art by Alitha E. Martinez

#4: *Under His Spell*
Story by Marie P. Croall; art by Hyeondo Park

#5: *I Date Dead People*
Story by Ann Kerns; art by Janina Görrissen

EDUCATIONAL TIE-INS:

Folklore; Relationships

HEADS UP:

Contains some instances of kissing, realistic violence, and death.

"WHAT'S NEXT ..."

MIKI FALLS SERIES
Story and art by Mark Crilley

A full list of titles appears on page 246.

HarperCollins, 2007-2008
Black and white, 176 pages each

Miki falls hard for new boy in school Hiro, but he hides a dangerous secret and a covert mission that threatens their chance at happiness. Middle-school readers who love forbidden paranormal romances will swoon over Crilley's manga-inspired series.

60

Olympians series

Story and art by George O'Connor

First Second, 2009-2012
Color, 80 pages each

When Rhea hid her son from Kronos, lord of the universe, she set into motion the fall of the Titans and the rise of the gods of Olympus, led by Zeus, god of thunder and lightning. Zeus bore many children, establishing the next generation of Olympians. Athena, goddess of wisdom, was one of Zeus' children who punished mortals for their foolish pride and rewarded heroes for their bravery. Zeus eventually took a bride, Hera, queen of the gods, and would forever cope with her jealousy and spite toward his children, including the hero Heracles. As one of three brothers, Zeus knew Hades' jealousy but never expected him to kidnap his daughter, holding her captive in the underworld.

Using primary sources to retell classic Greek myths, O'Connor's series is not only accurate but also action-packed and will appeal instantly to fans of mythology. Readers unfamiliar with the original stories will pick up this series easily, with its heavy super-hero styling and snappy modern dialogue. O'Connor's art is both dynamic and moody, fitting for stories about larger-than-life gods, and he manages to depict the more unsavory story elements in an age-appropriate manner. Each book focuses only on one particular god or goddess, but readers will be introduced to a whole range of characters, including other deities, monsters, creatures, heroes, and mortals. O'Connor has added tons of extras that will appeal to educators, including trading-card style profiles of the major characters, a family tree that grows with each new volume, discussion questions, and a further reading list.

IN THIS SERIES:

A full list of titles appears on page 247.

EDUCATIONAL TIE-INS:

Mythology; Gods and goddesses; Heroes

HEADS UP:

Contains instances of realistic violence and death.

"WHAT'S NEXT ..."

PERCY JACKSON AND THE OLYMPIANS: THE LIGHTNING THIEF: THE GRAPHIC NOVEL
Story by Rick Riordan and Robert Venditti
Art by Attila Futaki

Hyperion, 2010
Color, 128 pages

Based on the first book of the popular prose-novel series, *The Lightning Thief* is a perfect leap from O'Connor's retellings of ancient Greek myths to a fictional story featuring Greek gods. Discovering he is the son of Poseidon, Percy is recruited to a camp for demi-gods, where he learns that someone has stolen Zeus' powerful lightning bolt.

Possessions series

Story and art by Ray Fawkes

Oni Press, 2010-2012
Black and white with green (Book 1)
Black and white with blue (Book 2)
Black and white with pink (Book 3)
80 pages each

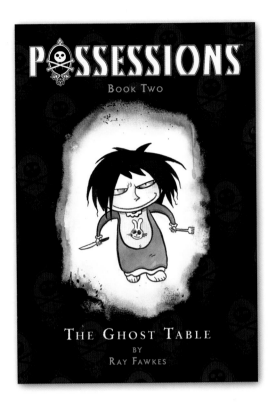

Gurgazon the Unclean may *look* like a 5-year-old girl, but she is actually an evil pit demon. Trapped in the Llewellyn-Vane House for Captured Spirits and Ghostly Curiosities, Gurgazon has little opportunity to be evil. But, with the help of the other inmates — the Ice Field Lights, the headless Pale Lady, the Sturmann Poltergeist aka "Polly," and the haunted jukebox named Duke — Gurgazon attempts to escape but must first get past the mysterious and seemingly immortal butler Mr. Thorne.

Fawkes' horror series overflows with sarcasm, making it the perfect series for readers who like their scares to be snarky, funny, and just a touch offbeat. The first volume introduces the characters, but, as the series continues, Fawkes gives readers more details about how each inmate arrived, all wrapped up in Gurgazon's elaborate and ongoing attempts to escape. The art is loose and often exaggerated, playing up the humor. Fawkes doesn't shy away from gross-out moments (including Gurgazon's fondness for projectile vomit), but the main theme of the series is the friendships these lost souls build with each other.

IN THIS SERIES:

Book One: Unclean Getaway
Book Two: The Ghost Table
Book Three: The Better House Trap

EDUCATIONAL TIE-INS:

Friendship; Folklore

HEADS UP:

Contains multiple instances of cartoon violence, potty humor, and name-calling.

"WHAT'S NEXT ..."

THE MIGHTY SKULLBOY ARMY SERIES
Story and art by Jacob Chabot

A full list of titles appears on page 247.
Dark Horse, 2007-2012
Black and white, 88-128 pages

For more fun with sarcastic anti-heroes, readers should pick up Chabot's silly action series about Skullboy (an elementary-school-age CEO of an evil corporation) and his henchmen Unit 1 (a robot) and Unit 2 (a monkey who may or may not be a genius).

Power Pack Classic Vol. 1

Story by Louise Simonson
Art by June Brigman, Bob Wiacek, and others

Marvel, 2009
Color, 256 pages

The Power children — Alex, Julie, Jack, and Katie — are rescued by an alien named Aelfyre Whitemane (also known as Whitey), after a race of lizard-like aliens called Snarks kidnap their parents. Whitey explains about their father's research into matter/anti-matter conversion and how The Snarks want to use his formula as a weapon to rule the galaxy. Mortally wounded, Whitey transfers each of his powers to the four children so that they can rescue their parents and save the world from destruction. In their new role as super-heroes, the children protect each other, work with other super-heroes, and practice their powers while trying to keep them secret from their parents.

First published as a comic-book series in the 1980s, *Power Pack* is still relevant today, with its stories of super-powered kids acting independently from their parents, taking risks, and learning how to control their special abilities — all popular elements in much of today's children's fiction. Simonson writes children as children with realistic dialogue, sibling friction, and authentic reactions to both the extraordinary and the mundane events in their lives. Brigman's art leans on the traditional super-hero side but features clean lines and strong facial expressions. This volume is a good introduction to other Marvel characters with a guest appearance by Spider-Man along with such lesser-known heroes as Cloak and Dagger. Subsequent volumes include more guest stars, but parents should note that later volumes do contain more mature content.

EDUCATIONAL TIE-INS:
Independence; Aliens; Heroes; Real-life issues

HEADS UP:
Contains some instances of realistic violence.

"WHAT'S NEXT ..."

TAKIO
Story by Brian Michael Bendis
Art by Michael Avon Oeming

Marvel/Icon, 2011
Color, 96 pages

Readers looking for more stories about kids and their discovery of super-powers may enjoy Bendis and Oeming's story of two sisters who are caught in a freak accident, gain telekinetic powers, and decide to become super-heroes.

ADVENTURE • HISTORICAL FICTION

Resistance series

Story by Carla Jablonski
Art by Leland Purvis
Colors by Hilary Sycamore

First Second, 2010-2012
Color, 128 pages

With the German Army occupying much of France, life for Paul and his little sister Marie will never be the same. They have no word from their prisoner-of-war father. Their older sister is flirting with Nazis to get information to pass to her boyfriend in the French Resistance. The soldiers keep stealing from their family's vineyard. And their friend Henri is in danger because he is Jewish. The siblings must work together to save Henri and to help the Resistance in any way they can.

Jablonski's gripping, realistic story will have kids instantly identifying with Paul and Marie, and the readers will understand the characters' fear and determination to help. Purvis is skilled at using the graphic-novel medium to tell a story, allowing his drawings of the characters, as well as Paul's drawings from his sketchbook, to paint a picture of a tense time. *Resistance* is not only great for classroom studies of World War II, it is also engaging historical fiction. Violence and death are part of the tale but do not overwhelm the story. Instead, readers are left with a believable sense of the suffocating danger of life during the French Resistance.

IN THIS SERIES:

Book 1: Resistance
Book 2: Defiance
Book 3: Victory

AWARDS:

2011 Young Adult Library Services Association Great Graphic Novel for Teens List (*Resistance*); 2011 Association of Jewish Libraries Sydney Taylor Honor for Older Readers (*Resistance*)

EDUCATIONAL TIE-INS:

World War II – French Resistance, German occupation, Holocaust; Art and artists; Discussion guides available at *http://media.us.macmillan.com/ readersguides/9781596432918RG.pdf* (*Resistance*) and *http://media.us.macmillan.com/readersguides/ 9781596432925RG.pdf* (*Defiance*)

HEADS UP:

Contains instances of realistic violence and death, as well as strong, frightening, or mature scenes.

"WHAT'S NEXT ..."

A FAMILY SECRET
Story and art by Eric Heuvel
Translation by Lorraine Miller

THE SEARCH
Story by Eric Heuvel, Ruud van der Rol, and Lies Schippers
Translation by Lorraine Miller

Farrar, Straus and Giroux Books for Young Readers, 2009
Color, 64 pages each

ANNE FRANK: THE ANNE FRANK HOUSE AUTHORIZED GRAPHIC BIOGRAPHY
Story by Sid Jacobson
Art by Ernie Colón

Farrar, Straus and Giroux/Hill and Wang, 2010
Color, 160 pages

For more fictional accounts of World War II and the Holocaust, readers can turn to Heuvel's interconnected graphic novels that tell the story of modern boy Jeoren learning about the experiences of his grandmother and friend during the German occupation of the Netherlands. For a nonfiction approach, try Jacobson and Colón's biography of teen Holocaust diarist Anne Frank. All three titles were created with the assistance of The Anne Frank House in Amsterdam.

39

Shazam! The Monster Society of Evil

Story and art by Jeff Smith
Colors by Steve Hamaker

DC Comics, 2007
Color, 208 pages

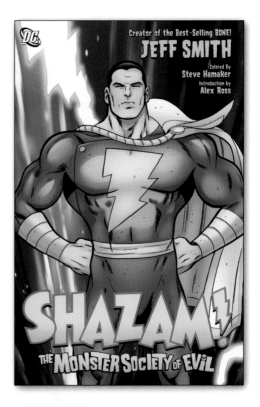

Billy Batson, an orphan living in an abandoned building, is led to an ancient cave, where a wizard grants him the powers of the heroes of myth. By saying the magic word "Shazam," Billy transforms into Captain Marvel. Returning home with his new-found powers, Captain Marvel protects his city from danger but also attracts the attention of Dr. Sivana, a corrupt government official. When giant robots under the control of the evil Mr. Mind appear and threaten to eliminate human civilization, Captain Marvel must find a way to defeat them and rescue his newly discovered sister from the hands of Dr. Sivana.

Known mainly for his work on *Bone*, Smith updates a classic super-hero for a modern audience. Readers will relish the wonder of a young boy gaining extraordinary powers and enjoy the dynamic super-hero action throughout the book. Beginning on a darker note, as the homeless Billy is attacked by a street thug, *Shazam!* quickly veers into brightly colored action sequences and a strong message about the importance of family, as Billy and his sister are reunited. Young readers with a fondness for mythology will enjoy the references to various heroes, both Greek and Roman.

EDUCATIONAL TIE-INS:

Mythology; Reporters; the Media; Family; Responsibility

HEADS UP:

Contains some instances of realistic violence, mature themes, and strong language.

"WHAT'S NEXT ..."

BATMAN: THE BRAVE AND THE BOLD SERIES
Story and art by various

THE BRAVE AND THE BOLD
THE FEARSOME FANG STRIKES AGAIN
EMERALD KNIGHT

DC Comics, 2010-2011
Color, 128 pages each

Readers who enjoyed the age-appropriate, super-hero action in Smith's updated Captain Marvel tale should check out this series of super-hero team-ups starring Batman and other characters from DC Comics. Such well-known characters as Green Lantern are featured along with more obscure ones — and Captain Marvel makes an appearance in the first volume.

Smile

Story and art by Raina Telgemeier
Colors by Stephanie Yue

Scholastic/Graphix, 2010
Color, 218 pages

In sixth grade, Raina falls and damages her two front teeth, leaving her facing years of braces, surgeries, and dental work. As if that weren't bad enough, she also has middle school to contend with: friends who turn mean, crushes on a boy who doesn't notice her, and puberty. But a love of art and the discovery of her own inner strength will help her get through anything.

Telgemeier bares both her dental troubles and her young-teen problems in an autobiography that will ring true to anyone currently stuck in middle school, as well to those who have survived. Though her story is set in the early 1990s, it has a timeless quality that keeps it from feeling dated. Such issues as puberty are touched on enough to be realistic but are not the focus of the work. The eye-catching cover and open, friendly art make this a gender-neutral pick that boys will also enjoy.

AWARDS:

2011 Will Eisner Comic Industry Award for Best Publication for Teens; 2011 Young Adult Library Services Association Great Graphic Novel for Teens List — Top Ten; 2011 Association for Library Service to Children Notable Children's Book; 2010 Boston Globe-Horn Book Honor for Nonfiction

EDUCATIONAL TIE-INS:

Self-esteem; Puberty; Art and artists; Autobiographies

From the *New York Times* Bestselling Author
Raina Telgemeier

Smile

HEADS UP:

Contains minor kissing and discussion of issues related to puberty.

"WHAT'S NEXT ..."

PAGE BY PAIGE
Story and art by Laura Lee Gulledge

Abrams/Amulet, 2011
Black and white, 192 pages

Older middle-schoolers might enjoy this slightly more mature take on the coming-of-age artist story.

91

© 2010 Raina Telgemeier

The Storm in the Barn

Story and art by Matt Phelan

Candlewick, 2009
Color, 208 pages

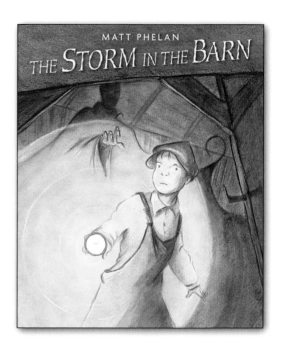

In addition to dealing with the anguish of living during the Dust Bowl of the 1930s in Kansas, 11-year-old Jack contends with bullies, his ill sister, and his father's disappointment in him. Jack tries his best to make himself useful but only manages to make people believe that he may be suffering from "dust dementia." Sensing something strange in the neighbor's abandoned barn, Jack investigates until he comes face to face with a supernatural creature that he must defeat to prove his courage and end the drought.

Phelan blends history and fantasy in this tall-tale-inspired story that will appeal to fans of both genres. He has created an intriguing supernatural villain in the King of Storms that feels as if it has leapt from the pages of American folklore. As a boy thrust into this world, Jack is powerless, and readers will cheer for his accomplishments and relate to his search for his role in his family. Despite the book's historical context and serious, quiet tone, it makes for fast-paced reading, with many wordless sequences and tons of action. Phelan's moody watercolor art suits Dust Bowl-era Kansas and quickly gives the reader a sense of place.

AWARDS:

2010 Scott O'Dell Award for Historical Fiction

EDUCATIONAL TIE-INS:

Dust Bowl; Tall tales; Family; Courage

HEADS UP:

Contains a few strong or frightening scenes.

"WHAT'S NEXT ..."

WONDERSTRUCK
Story and art by Brian Selznick

Scholastic Press, 2011
Black and white, 640 pages

Rooted in real historical events, Selznick's part illustrated novel and part prose story is a good companion to Phelan's graphic novel, sharing the same strong sense of place and a similarly quiet tone. Although there is no fantasy element to *Wonderstruck*, readers who enjoy stories of self-discovery, curiosity, and a thirst for independence will see common themes in both books.

SUPER-HERO

Superman: Secret Origin

Story by Geoff Johns
Art by Gary Frank and Jon Sibal
Colors by Brad Anderson

DC Comics, 2010
Color, 224 pages

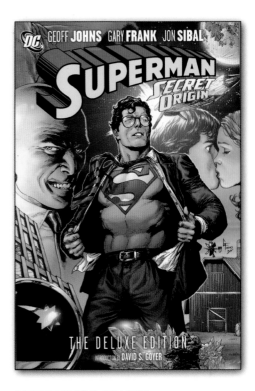

Before he was Superman, teenage Clark Kent lived in Smallville: coping with his increasingly powerful abilities, learning his true alien heritage, trying to fit in at school, and dealing with a bully named Lex Luthor. A group of teen super-heroes from the future show Clark his destiny as one of the greatest super-heroes ever, motivating him to move to Metropolis to become a newspaper reporter for *The Daily Planet*. On his first assignment accompanying star journalist Lois Lane to uncover the shadowy dealings of Luthor, Superman reveals himself for the first time to stop a rogue robot, raising suspicions from both the U.S. Army and the diabolical Luthor.

Johns' version of Superman's familiar origins makes the super-hero a more accessible character. He writes Clark Kent as a conflicted teen, not only dealing with such common issues as his crush on Lana Lang, but also with his anxiety of losing control of his powers or revealing them to others. Johns' story features plenty of super-hero action balanced with emotional character moments, and Frank's highly detailed art is larger than life: perfect for a story about Superman. This story introduces readers to all the major players in the Superman mythology along with such lesser-known ones as The Legion of Super-Heroes, Metallo, and The Parasite. As a self-contained story, *Secret Origin* is a good introduction to DC's most popular character.

EDUCATIONAL TIE-INS:
Heroes; Growing up

HEADS UP:
Contains some instances of realistic violence.

"WHAT'S NEXT ..."

ULTIMATE SPIDER-MAN VOL. 1: POWER AND RESPONSIBILITY
Story by Brian Michael Bendis
Art by Mark Bagley

Marvel, 2009
Color, 200 pages

Readers who enjoy Johns' new take on Superman's origin may like the modernization of Spider-Man's origin story. Bendis and Bagley keep the emotional impact of Peter Parker's transformation from science geek to spider-enhanced super-hero in a fast-paced, visually striking new take on this hero's beginnings. While this first volume is appropriate for middle-school readers, subsequent volumes do contain mature content.

Twin Spica series

Story and art by Kou Yaginuma
Translation by Maya Rosewood

Vertical, 2010-2012
Black and white, 192-288 pages

Since she was a little girl, Asumi dreamed of being a spacecraft pilot. Fourteen years after the disastrous crash of its first manned spacecraft, *The Lion*, Japan's space program opens the first space academy for teenagers, Tokyo Space School. Asumi is accepted, along with a small group of other students, and must face classroom studies, daily physical exercise, and rigorous space training. Still deeply affected by the crash of *The Lion*, the students find that it is only together that they can begin to heal.

Yaginuma's moving series touches many issues, including the loss of a parent, the psychological effects of major disasters, illness, cloning, identity, relationships, familial expectations, and more. Using realistic characters and a near-future setting, he creates a story that readers will feel is real and immediate. Readers thinking about their dreams and aspirations will easily identify with Asumi and her friends. Yaginuma's art is softly rounded, giving a gentle quality to the story. Non-science-fiction readers will enjoy the way that a ghost, nicknamed "Mr. Lion" by Asumi, ties the characters together and helps them handle the problems they encounter, while science-fiction fans will love the idea of a school for teenage astronauts.

IN THIS SERIES:

A full list of titles appears on page 250.

AWARDS:

2011 Young Adult Library Services Association Great Graphic Novel for Teens List

EDUCATIONAL TIE-INS:

Loss of a parent; Science; Astronauts; Careers

HEADS UP:

Contains minor instances of realistic violence and death. Story reads right-to-left.

"WHAT'S NEXT ..."

SATURN APARTMENTS SERIES

Story and art by Hisae Iwaoka
Translation by Matt Thorn

A full list of titles appears on page 250.

Viz, 2010-2012
Black and white, 192 pages each

Twin Spica fans who want to read another contemplative science-fiction series might like Iwaoka's story about a young window-washer who works on the Earth-orbiting space station on which all humans now live. Like *Twin Spica*, *Saturn Apartments* tells the story of a quiet protagonist and contrasts the everyday things that happen in his life with hints of greater political and cultural upheaval.

FANTASY • HUMOR • ROMANCE • SCHOOL & FAMILY

Ultra Maniac series

Story and art by Wataru Yoshizumi
Translation by Koji Goto

Viz, 2005-2006
Black and white, 184 pages each

Ayu is determined to present herself as calm, cool, and collected in order to catch the attention of Tetsushi, who admires girls who don't get upset easily. When she meets Nina, the new girl at school, Ayu discovers that her new friend is a witch who flunked out of magic school and was sent to the human world for remedial study. Touched by Ayu's friendship, Nina decides to help Ayu catch Tetsushi's eye using her magic, except that every spell produces disastrous yet hilarious results. The two girls must work together to keep Nina's magic from ruining everyone's love life.

Yoshizumi's sweet, silly series is a terrific introduction to the "magical girl" subgenre found in manga. The fantasy elements are mild and used mainly for comedic effect. Young readers who are beginning to explore their own pre-teen romances will identify with the touching relationships these middle-school characters experience. Readers will find a lot of blushing and handholding and a few kisses to sweeten the story. Other than one scene where Nina's magic transforms her and Ayu into adults in order to enter a nightclub, there is little mature content. The gently rounded art is light and airy and lots of fun, just like the plot.

IN THIS SERIES:

A full list of titles appears on page 250.

EDUCATIONAL TIE-INS:

Friendship, Self-esteem, Bullying
(*Volumes 3* and *4*)

HEADS UP:

Contains several instances of kissing and one instance of characters aged to adulthood wearing skimpy outfits and acting tipsy. Story reads right-to-left.

"WHAT'S NEXT ..."

SAILOR MOON SERIES
Story and art by Naoko Takeuchi

A full list of titles appears on page 251.

Kodansha, 2011-2012
Black and white, 208-244 pages

Ultra Maniac fans who want a slightly more mature magical girl title should try *Sailor Moon*, which was partly responsible for attracting American girls and women to manga when it was originally released in North America in 1997. Takeuchi's bouncy story about air-headed middle-school girl Usagi who can transform into the crime-stopping heroine Sailor Moon can now be read by a new generation.

CARDCAPTOR SAKURA SERIES
Story and art by Clamp
Translation by Mika Onishi and Anita Sengupta

A full list of titles appears on page 251.

Dark Horse, 2010-2012
Black and white, 576-600 pages

Cardcaptor Sakura will appeal to readers who liked the fun, chaotic effects that magic had on the characters in *Ultra Maniac* but who want even more fantasy elements. When Sakura opens a magical book in her father's library, she becomes the Cardcaptor, responsible for finding the Clow Cards that escaped from the book and returning them to their place before they cause too much damage to the real world.

Ultra Maniac © 2001 by Wataru Yoshizumi/Shjueisha Inc.

ADVENTURE • FANTASY

The Unsinkable Walker Bean

Story and art by Aaron Renier

First Second, 2010
Color, 208 pages

When his grandfather falls ill from the deadly magic of a cursed skull, reluctant hero Walker Bean must set off on a quest to return the skull to its rightful owners: a pair of ancient merwitches. Both Walker's father and the mysterious Dr. Patches refuse to let Walker leave with the skull, but he steals it and ends up on a pirate ship as a stowaway. Walker is unable to hide for long, and the pirates discover the skull and refuse to listen to Walker's warnings about its fatal powers, leaving the ship's captain on death's door. Now, with Dr. Patches on the pirate ship and the rest of the crew still refusing to believe that the skull is cursed, Walker must outwit everyone to return the skull to the merwitches before they find and destroy them all.

Renier's traditional adventure story with epic fantasy elements will appeal to readers looking for a book with depth and those who are fans of more involved high-fantasy stories. With a perfect mix of suspense, mystery, and strangeness, this tale is highly imaginative, from creepy-looking merwitches to steampunk-inspired contraptions that Walker's grandfather invents. Readers will cheer for Walker, as he develops from a meek, bookish boy into a capable leader who uses brains and strategy to outsmart everyone around him. Renier's detailed art requires close attention from readers, often including subtle details that are important to the story. The fast-paced nature of this book and its many unresolved clues will have readers demanding further volumes.

AWARDS:

2011 Young Adult Library Services Association Great Graphic Novel for Teens List

EDUCATIONAL TIE-INS:

Pirates; Quest stories; Friendship; Responsibility

HEADS UP:

Contains some instances of alcohol use by adults and realistic violence.

"WHAT'S NEXT ..."

POLLY AND THE PIRATES
Story and art by Ted Naifeh

Oni Press, 2006
Black and white, 176 pages

Readers who enjoy Walker's development into a strong leader and the heavy pirate element of Renier's book may wish to try out Naifeh's girl-pirate adventure. Prim and proper Polly's kidnapping leads to the discovery that her mother was a famous and dangerous pirate and that she has her own inner adventurer.

NEW BRIGHTON ARCHEOLOGICAL SOCIETY
Story by Mark Andrew Smith
Art by Matthew Weldon

Image, 2009
Color, 179 pages

When their parents go missing while on an archeological dig, two sets of siblings must do digging of their own — into their parents' mysterious past to discover the magical secrets they've kept hidden. Just as in *Unsinkable Walker Bean*, magic and family history combine to form an exciting adventure.

93

TITLE INFORMATION

BENNY AND PENNY SERIES

Story and art by Geoffrey Hayes

Benny and Penny in Just Pretend
Hardcover 978-0979923807 $12.95
Benny and Penny in The Big No-No!
Hardcover 978-0979923890 $12.95
Benny and Penny in The Toy Breaker
Hardcover 978-1935179078 $12.95
Toon Books, 2008-2011
Color, 32 pages each

BENNY AND PENNY WHAT'S NEXT ...

A Couple of Boys Have the Best Week Ever
Story and art by Marla Frazee

Hardcover 978-0152060206 $16.99
Harcourt, 2008
Color, 40 pages

CAPTAIN RAPTOR SERIES

Story by Kevin O'Malley
Art by Patrick O'Brien

Captain Raptor and the Moon Mystery
Hardcover 978-0802789358 $16.95
Captain Raptor and the Space Pirates
Hardcover 978-0802795717 $16.95
Walker, 2005, 2007
Color, 32 pages each

CAPTAIN RAPTOR WHAT'S NEXT ...

Once upon a Cool Motorcycle Dude
Story by Kevin O'Malley
Art by Kevin O'Malley, Carol Heyer,
and Scott Goto

Hardcover 978-0802789471 $16.95
Walker Books for Young Readers, 2005
Color, 32 pages

Once upon a Royal Super Baby
Story by Kevin O'Malley
Art by Kevin O'Malley, Carol Heyer,
and Scott Goto

Hardcover 978-0802721648 $16.99
Walker Books for Young Readers, 2010
Color, 32 pages

DESPERATE DOG SERIES

Story and art by Eileen Christelow

Letters from a Desperate Dog
Hardcover 978-0618510030 $16.00
The Desperate Dog Writes Again
Hardcover 978-0547242057 $16.99
Clarion Books, 2005; 2010
Color, 32 pages each

DESPERATE DOG WHAT'S NEXT ...

Doggie Dreams
Story and art by Mike Herrod
Hardcover 978-1609050658 $10.99
Blue Apple Books, 2011
Color, 40 pages

DETECTIVE BLUE

Story by Steve Metzger
Art by Tedd Arnold

Hardcover 978-0545172868 $16.99
Scholastic/Orchard Books, 2011
Color, 32 pages

DETECTIVE BLUE WHAT'S NEXT ...

The Three Pigs
Story and art by David Wiesner

Hardcover 978-0618007011 $16.99
Clarion Books, 2001
Color, 40 pages

Hector Protector and As I Went over the Water: Two Nursery Rhymes with Pictures
Story and art by Maurice Sendak

Hardcover 978-0060286422 $19.95
HarperCollins, 2011
Color, 64 pages

ELEPHANT & PIGGIE SERIES

Story and art by Mo Willems

Today I Will Fly!
Hardcover 978-1423102953 $8.99

My Friend Is Sad
Hardcover 978-1423102977 $8.99

There Is a Bird on Your Head!
Hardcover 978-1423106869 $8.99

I Am Invited to a Party!
Hardcover 978-1423106876 $8.99

I Love My New Toy!
Hardcover 978-1423109617 $8.99

I Will Surprise My Friend!
Hardcover 978-1423109624 $8.99

Are You Ready to Play Outside?
Hardcover 978-1423113478 $8.99

Watch Me Throw the Ball!
Hardcover 978-1423113485 $8.99

Elephants Cannot Dance!
Hardcover 978-1423114109 $8.99

Pigs Make Me Sneeze!
Hardcover 978-1423114116 $8.99

I Am Going!
Hardcover 978-1423119906 $8.99

Can I Play Too?
Hardcover 978-1423119913 $8.99

We Are in a Book!
Hardcover 978-1423133087 $8.99

I Broke My Trunk!
Hardcover 978-1423133094 $8.99

Should I Share My Ice Cream?
Hardcover 978-1423143437 $8.99

Happy Pig Day!
Hardcover 978-1423143420 $8.99
Hyperion Books, 2007-2011
Color, 64 pages each

ELEPHANT & PIGGIE WHAT'S NEXT ...

Hippo and Rabbit series
Story and art by Jeff Mack

Three Short Tales
Paperback 978-0545274456 $3.99

Brave Like Me
Paperback 978-0545274456 $3.99
Scholastic/Cartwheel Books, 2011
Color, 32 pages each

HOCUS POCUS

Story by Sylvie Desrosiers
Art by Remy Simard

Hardcover 978-1554535774 $16.95
Kids Can Press, 2011
Color, 32 pages

HOCUS POCUS WHAT'S NEXT ...

Octopus Soup
Story and art by Mercer Mayer

Hardcover 978-0761458128 $16.99
Marshall Cavendish, 2011
Color, 32 pages

IN THE NIGHT KITCHEN

Story and art by Maurice Sendak

Hardcover, 978-0060266684 $17.95
Paperback, 978-0064434362 $7.95
HarperCollins, 1970
Color, 40 pages

IN THE NIGHT KITCHEN WHAT'S NEXT ...

Tuesday
Story and art by David Wiesner

Hardcover 978-0395551134 $17.00
Paperback 978-0395870822 $7.99
Clarion Books, 1991
Color, 32 pages

JOHNNY BOO SERIES

Story and art by James Kochalka

The Best Little Ghost in the World
Hardcover 978-1603090131 $9.95

Twinkle Power
Hardcover 978-1603090155 $9.95

Happy Apples
Hardcover 978-1603090414 $9.95

The Mean Little Boy

Hardcover 978-1603090599 $9.95

Does Something!
Hardcover 978-1603090841 $9.95
Top Shelf, 2008-2012
Color, 40 pages each

JOHNNY BOO WHAT'S NEXT ...

Otto's Orange Day
Story by Jay Lynch
Art by Frank Cammuso

Hardcover 978-0979923821 $12.95
Toon Books, 2008
Color, 40 pages

KAPOW!; KER-SPLASH! SERIES

Story and art by George O'Connor

Kapow!
Paperback 978-1416968474 $12.99
Ker-splash!
Paperback 978-1442421967 $19.99
Simon & Schuster/Aladdin, 2007, 2010
Color, 48 pages and 40 pages

KAPOW!; KER-SPLASH! WHAT'S NEXT ...

Batman: The Story of the Dark Knight
Hardcover 978-0670062553 $16.99
Superman: The Story of the Man of Steel
Hardcover 978-0670062850 $16.99
Wonder Woman: The Story of the Amazon Princess
Hardcover 978-0670062560 $16.99
Story and art by Ralph Cosentino

Viking Juvenile, 2008-2011
Color, 40 pages each

LITTLE MOUSE GETS READY

Story and art by Jeff Smith

Hardcover 978-0759531451 $12.95
Toon Books, 2009
Color, 32 pages

LITTLE MOUSE GETS READY WHAT'S NEXT ...

Billy Tartle in Say Cheese!
Story and art by Michael Townsend

Hardcover 978-0375839320 $15.99
Knopf, 2007
Color, 40 pages

Cat the Cat series
Story and art by Mo Willems

Cat the Cat Who Is That?
Hardcover 978-0061728402 $10.99
What's Your Sound Hound the Hound?
Hardcover 978-0061728440 $10.99
Let's Say Hi to Friends That Fly
Hardcover 978-0061728426 $10.99
Time to Sleep Sheep the Sheep
Hardcover 978-0061728471 $10.99
Balzer and Bray, 2010
Color, 32 pages each

LUKE ON THE LOOSE

Story and art by Harry Bliss

Hardcover 978-1935179009 $12.95
Toon Books, 2009
Color, 32 pages

LUKE ON THE LOOSE WHAT'S NEXT ...

The Puddleman
Story and art by Raymond Briggs

Paperback 978-0099456421 $7.99
Red Fox, 2004
Color, 32 pages

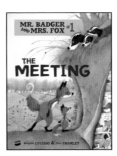

MR. BADGER AND MRS. FOX SERIES

Story by Brigitte Luciani
Art by Eve Tharlet
Translation by Carol Klio Burrell

#1: The Meeting
Paperback 978-0761356318 $6.95
#2: A Hubbub
Paperback 978-0761356325 $6.95
#3: What a Team!
Paperback 978-0761356332 $6.95
Lerner/Graphic Universe, 2010, 2011
Color, 32 pages each

MR. BADGER AND MRS. FOX WHAT'S NEXT ...

Patrick in a Teddy Bear's Picnic and Other Stories
Story and art by Geoffrey Hayes

Hardcover 978-1935179092 $12.95
Toon Books, 2011
Color, 32 pages

OWLY SERIES

Story and art by Andy Runton

The Way Home & The Bittersweet Summer
Paperback 978-1891830624 $10
Just a Little Blue
Paperback 978-1891830648 $10
Flying Lessons
Paperback 978-1891830761 $10
A Time to Be Brave
Paperback 978-1891830891 $10
Tiny Tales
Paperback 978-1603090193 $10
Top Shelf, 2004-2008
Black and white, 120-160 pages
Owly & Wormy: Friends All Aflutter
Hardcover 978-1416957744 $15.99
Simon & Schuster/Atheneum, 2011
Color, 40 pages

OWLY WHAT'S NEXT ...

Chicken and Cat
Story and art by Sara Varon
Hardcover 978-0439634069 $16.99
Scholastic, 2006
Color, 40 pages

Chicken and Cat Clean Up
Story and art by Sara Varon
Hardcover 978-0439634083 $16.99
Scholastic, 2009
Color, 48 pages

RICK & RACK AND THE GREAT OUTDOORS

Story and art by Ethan Long
Hardcover 978-1609050344 $10.99
Blue Apple Books, 2010
Color, 40 pages

RICK & RACK AND THE GREAT OUTDOORS WHAT'S NEXT ...

Benjamin Bear in Fuzzy Thinking
Story and art by Philippe Coudray
Hardcover 978-1935179122 $12.95
Toon Books, 2011
Color, 32 pages
Lucky Leaf
Story and art by Kevin O'Malley
Paperback 978-0802796479 $7.99
Walker, 2005
Color, 32 pages

SILLY LILLY SERIES

Story and art by Agnes Rosenstiehl

Silly Lilly and the Four Seasons
Hardcover 978-1442445383 $19.99
Silly Lilly in What Will I Be Today?
Hardcover 978-1442445390 $19.99
Toon Books, 2008, 2010
Color, 32 pages each

SILLY LILLY WHAT'S NEXT ...

Yo Gabba Gabba! series
Good Night, Gabbaland
Story by J. Torres
Art by Matthew Loux
Board Book 978-1934964569 $7.99
Oni Press, 2010
Color, 16 pages

Gabba Ball
Story and art by Chris Eliopoulos
Board Book 978-1934964552 $7.99
Oni Press, 2010
Color, 16 pages

My Name is Elizabeth
Story by Annika Dunklee
Art by Matt Forsythe
Hardcover 978-1554535606 $14.95
Kids Can Press, 2011
Color, 32 pages

ZOE AND ROBOT: LET'S PRETEND!
Story and art by Ryan Sias
Hardcover 978-1609050634 $10.99
Blue Apple Books, 2011
Color, 40 pages

ZOE AND ROBOT: LET'S PRETEND! WHAT'S NEXT ...

Cat Secrets
Story and art by Jeff Czekaj
Hardcover 978-0061920882 $16.99
Balzer + Bray, 2011
Color, 32 pages

Traction Man series
Story and art by Mini Grey

Traction Man is Here!
Hardcover 978-0375831911 $16.99

Traction Man Meets Turbo Dog
Hardcover 978-0375855832 $16.99
Knopf, 2005, 2008
Color, 32 pages each

THE SNOWMAN
Story and art by Raymond Briggs
Paperback 978-0394884660 $6.99
Random House/Dragonfly Books, 1986
Color, 32 pages

THE SNOWMAN WHAT'S NEXT ...

The Adventures of Polo series
Story and art by Regis Faller

The Adventures of Polo
Hardcover 978-1596431607 $17.95

Polo: The Runaway Book
Hardcover 978-1596431898 $16.95
Roaring Brook Press, 2006-2007
Color, 80 pages each

THE ADVENTURES OF DANIEL BOOM, AKA LOUD BOY SERIES

Story by D.J. Steinberg
Art by Brian Smith

#1: Sound Off!
Paperback 978-0448446981 $5.99
#2: Mac Attack!
Paperback 978-0448446998 $5.99
#3: Game On!
Paperback 978-0448447001 $5.99
#4: Grow Up!
Paperback 978-0448447018 $5.99
Penguin/Grosset & Dunlap, 2008-2010
Color, 96 pages each

THE ADVENTURES OF DANIEL BOOM, AKA LOUD BOY WHAT'S NEXT ...

Hyperactive
Story by Scott Christian Sava
Art by Joseph Bergin III

Paperback 978-1600103131 $12.99
IDW, 2008
Color, 112 pages

BABYMOUSE SERIES

Story by Jennifer L. Holm and Matthew Holm
Art by Matthew Holm

#1: Queen of the World
Hardcover 978-0375932298 $12.99
Paperback 978-0375832291 $5.95
#2: Our Hero
Hardcover 978-0375932304 $12.99
Paperback 978-0375832307 $5.95
#3: Beach Babe
Hardcover 978-0375932311 $12.99
Paperback 978-0375932311 $5.95
#4: Rock Star
Hardcover 978-0375932328 $12.99
Paperback 978-0375832321 $5.95
#5: Heartbreaker
Hardcover 978-0375937989 $12.99
Paperback 978-0375837982 $5.99
#6: Camp Babymouse
Hardcover 978-0375939884 $12.99
Paperback 978-0375839887 $5.99
#7: Skater Girl
Hardcover 978-0375939891 $12.99
Paperback 978-0375839894 $5.99
#8: Puppy Love
Hardcover 978-0375939907 $12.99
Paperback 978-0375839900 $5.99
#9: Monster Mash
Hardcover 978-0375937897 $12.99
Paperback 978-0375843877 $5.99
#10: The Musical
Hardcover 978-0375937910 $12.99
Paperback 978-0375843884 $5.99
#11: Dragonslayer
Hardcover 978-0375957123 $12.99
Paperback 978-0375857126 $5.99
#12: Burns Rubber
Hardcover 978-0375957130 $12.99
Paperback 978-0375857133 $6.99
#13: Cupcake Tycoon
Hardcover 978-0375965739 $12.99
Paperback 978-0375865732 $6.99
#14: Mad Scientist
Hardcover 978-0375965746 $12.99
Paperback 978-0375865749 $6.99
#15: A Very Babymouse Christmas
Hardcover 978-0375967795 $12.99
Paperback 978-0375867798 $6.99
Random House, 2005-2011
Black and white with pink (vol. 9 is black and white with orange), 96 pages each

BABYMOUSE WHAT'S NEXT ...

The Baby-sitters Club series

Story by Ann M. Martin
Adaptation and art by Raina Telgemeier

Kristy's Great Idea
Paperback 978-0439871655 $8.99
The Truth about Stacy
Paperback 978-0439739368 $8.99
Mary Anne Saves the Day
Paperback 978-0439885164 $8.99
Claudia and Mean Janine
Paperback 978-0439885171 $8.99
Scholastic/Graphix, 2005-2008
Black and white, 144-186 pages

BINKY SERIES

Story and art by Ashley Spires

Binky the Space Cat
Hardcover 978-1554533091 $16.95
Paperback 978-1554534197 $8.95
Binky to the Rescue
Hardcover 978-1554535026 $16.95
Paperback 978-1554535972 $8.95
Binky under Pressure
Hardcover 978-1554535040 $16.95
Paperback 978-1554537679 $8.95
Kids Can Press, 2009-2011
Color, 64 pages each

BINKY WHAT'S NEXT ...

The Adventures of Panda Man series
Story by Sho Makura
Art by Haruhi Kato

Panda Man to the Rescue!
Paperback 978-1421535203 $7.99
Panda Man and the Treasure Hunt
Paperback 978-1421535210 $7.99
Panda Man vs. Chiwanda
Paperback 978-1421535227 $7.99
Viz, 2010-2011
Black and white with color, 96 pages each

DRAGON PUNCHER SERIES

Story and art by James Kochalka

Book 1: Dragon Puncher
Hardcover 978-1603090575 $9.95
Book 2: Dragon Puncher Island
Hardcover 978-1603090858 $9.95
Top Shelf, 2010-2011
Color, 40 pages each

DRAGON PUNCHER WHAT'S NEXT ...

Tiger Moth series
Story by Aaron Reynolds
Art by Erik Lervold

Tiger Moth: Insect Ninja
Hardcover 978-1598890570 $22.95
Paperback 978-1598892284 $4.95
Tiger Moth: The Fortune Cookies of Weevil
Hardcover 978-1598893182 $22.65
Paperback 978-1598894134 $4.95
Tiger Moth: The Dung Beetle Bandits
Hardcover 978-1598893175 $22.65
Paperback 978-1598894127 $4.95
Tiger Moth: The Dragon Kite Contest
Hardcover 978-1598890563 $22.65
Paperback 978-1598892291 $4.95
Tiger Moth: Kung Pow Chicken
Hardcover 978-1434204554 $22.65
Paperback 978-1434205056 $4.95
Tiger Moth: The Pest Show on Earth
Hardcover 978-1434204547 $22.65
Paperback 978-1434205049 $4.95
Capstone/Stone Arch, 2007-2008
Color, 40 pages each
Tiger Moth: Adventures of an Insect Ninja compilation
Capstone/Stone Arch, 2011
Paperback 978-1434230324 $7.95
Color, 128 pages

FASHION KITTY SERIES

Story and art by Charise Mericle Harper

Fashion Kitty
Paperback 978-0786851348 $8.99

Fashion Kitty versus the Fashion Queen
Paperback 978-0786837267 $8.99

Fashion Kitty and the Unlikely Hero
Paperback 978-0786837274 $8.99

Fashion Kitty and the B.O.Y.S. (Ball of Yellow String) [a graphic-novel hybrid; part text, part comics]
Paperback 978-1423136545 $9.99
Disney/Hyperion, 2005-2011
Color, 96-112 pages

FASHION KITTY WHAT'S NEXT ...

Zoey Zeta and the Sisters of Power series
Story by Robert Simon
Art by Tomomi Sarafov

#1 Family Secrets
Paperback 978-0986539206 $8.99

#2 Army of Mean
Paperback 978-0986539244 $7.99
Zeta Comics, 2010-2011
Color, 50-52 pages

Princess Candy series
Story by Michael Dahl; Art by Jeff Crowther

Princess Candy: Sugar Hero
Hardcover 978-1434215871 $22.95
Paperback 978-1434228017 $4.95

Princess Candy: The Marshmallow Mermaid
Hardcover 978-1434215888 $22.65
Paperback 978-1434228024 $4.95

Princess Candy: The Green Queen of Mean
Hardcover 978-1434218933 $22.65
Paperback 978-1434228031 $4.95

Princess Candy: The Evil Echo
Hardcover 978-1434219770 $22.65
Paperback 978-1434228048 $4.95
Capstone/Stone Arch, 2010-2011
Color, 40 pages each

GABBY & GATOR

Story and art by James Burks
Hardcover 978-0759531451 $16.99
Yen Press, 2010
Color, 186 pages

GABBY & GATOR WHAT'S NEXT ...

Luz Sees the Light
Story and art by Claudia Davila
Hardcover 978-1554535811 $16.99
Paperback 978-1554537662 $8.95
Kids Can Press, 2011
Black and white with brown, 96 pages

Adopt a Glurb
Story and art by Elise Gravel
Hardcover 978-1609050375 $10.99
Blue Apple Books, 2010
Color, 40 pages

GERONIMO STILTON SERIES

Story by "Geronimo Stilton"
Concept by Elisabetta Dami
Art by Lorenzo de Pretto (#1 and #2), Ambrogio M. Piazzoni (#3), Wasabi Studio (#4), Giuseppe Facciotto (#5), Giuseppe Ferrario (#7), Federica Salfo (#8)
Graphics by Michaela Battaglin and Marta Lorini
Translation by Nanette McGuinness

#1: The Discovery of America
Hardcover 978-1597071581 $9.99

#2: The Secret of the Sphinx
Hardcover 978-1597071598 $9.99

#3: The Coliseum Con
Hardcover 978-1597071727 $9.99

#4: Following the Trail of Marco Polo
Hardcover 978-1597071888 $9.99

#5: The Great Ice Age
Hardcover 978-1597072021 $9.99

#6: Who Stole the Mona Lisa?
Hardcover 978-1597072212 $9.99

#7: Dinosaurs in Action!
Hardcover 978-1597072397 $9.99

#8: Play It Again, Mozart!
Hardcover 978-1597072762 $9.99

#9: The Weird Book Machine
Hardcover 978-1597072953 $9.99
NBM/Papercutz, 2009-2012
Color, 56 pages each

GERONIMO STILTON GRAPHIC NOVELS WHAT'S NEXT ...

Good Times Travel Agency series
Story by Linda Bailey
Art by Bill Slavin

Adventures in Ancient Egypt
Paperback 978-1550745481 $10.95

Adventures in the Middle Ages
Hardcover 978-1550745382 $14.95
Paperback 978-1550745405 $8.95

Adventures with the Vikings
Paperback 978-1550745443 $8.95

Adventures in Ancient Greece
Paperback 978-1550745368 $10.95

Adventures in Ancient China
Paperback 978-1553374541 $8.95

Adventures in the Ice Age
Paperback 978-1553375043 $8.95
Kids Can Press, 2000-2004
Color, 48 pages each

GUINEA PIG: PET SHOP PRIVATE EYE SERIES

Story by Colleen AF Venable
Art by Stephanie Yue

#1: Hamster and Cheese
Paperback 978-1421518053 $6.95

#2: And Then There Were Gnomes
Paperback 978-1421518053 $6.95

#3: The Ferret's a Foot
Paperback 978-1421518053 $6.95

#4: Fish You Were Here
Paperback 978-1421518053 $6.95
Lerner/Graphic Universe, 2010-2011
Color, 48 pages each

GUINEA PIG: PET SHOP PRIVATE EYE WHAT'S NEXT ...

Zig and Wikki in Something Ate My Homework
Story by Nadja Spiegelman
Art by Trade Loeffler

Hardcover 978-1935179023 $12.95
Toon Book, 2010
Color, 40 pages

KIT FEENY SERIES

Story and art by Michael Townsend

On the Move
Hardcover 978-0375956140 $12.99
Paperback 978-0375856143 $5.99

The Ugly Necklace
Hardcover 978-0375956157 $12.99
Paperback 978-0375856150 $5.99
Random House, 2009
Black and white with orange, 96 pages each

KIT FEENY WHAT'S NEXT ...

Frankie Pickle series
Story and art by Eric Wight

Frankie Pickle and the Closet of Doom
Hardcover 978-141696484 $9.99
Paperback 978-1442413047 $5.99

Frankie Pickle and the Pine Run 3000
Hardcover 978-1416964858 $9.99

Frankie Pickle and the Mathemagical Menace
Hardcover 978-1416989721 $9.99
Simon & Schuster, 2009-2011
Black and white, 96 pages each

LONG TAIL KITTY

Art and story by Lark Pien

Hardcover 978-1934706442 $14.99
Blue Apple Books, 2009
Color, 51 pages

LONG TAIL KITTY WHAT'S NEXT ...

The Super Crazy Cat Dance
Story and art by Aron Nels Steinke

Hardcover 978-1609050351 $10.99
Blue Apple Books, 2010
Color, 40 pages

LUNCH LADY SERIES

Story and art by Jarrett J. Krosoczka

And the Cyborg Substitute
Paperback 978-0375846830 $6.99
And the League of Librarians
Paperback 978-0375846847 $6.99
And the Author Visit Vendetta
Paperback 978-0375860942 $6.99
And the Summer Camp Shakedown
Paperback 978-0375860959 $6.99
And the Bake Sale Bandit
Paperback 978-0375867293 $6.99
And the Field Trip Fiasco
Paperback 978-0375867309 $6.99
Knopf, 2009-2011
Black and white with yellow, 96 pages each

LUNCH LADY WHAT'S NEXT ...

Magic Pickle
Story and art by Scott Morse
Paperback 978-0439879959 $9.99
Scholastic/Graphix, 2008
Color, 112 pages

MAGIC TRIXIE SERIES

Story and art by Jill Thompson
Lettering by Jason Arthur

Magic Trixie
Paperback 978-0061170454 $7.99
Magic Trixie Sleeps Over
Paperback 978-0061170485 $7.99
Magic Trixie and the Dragon
Paperback 978-0061170508 $7.99
HarperTrophy, 2008-2009
Color, 94 pages each

MAGIC TRIXIE WHAT'S NEXT ...

Sticky Burr series
Story and art by John Lechner

Adventures in Burrwood Forest
Paperback 978-0763635671 $6.99
The Prickly Peril
Paperback 978-0763645809 $6.99
Candlewick, 2008-2009
Color, 56 pages each

NURSERY RHYME COMICS: 50 TIMELESS RHYMES FROM 50 CELEBRATED CARTOONISTS

Art by various

Hardcover 978-1596436008 $18.99

First Second, 2011

Color, 120 pages

NURSERY RHYME COMICS: 50 TIMELESS RHYMES FROM 50 CELEBRATED CARTOONISTS WHAT'S NEXT ...

Graphic Spin series

Shivers, Wishes, and Wolves: Stone Arch Fairy Tales Volume One

Story and art by various

Paperback 978-1434230317 $12.95

Secrets, Monsters, and Magic Mirrors: Stone Arch Fairy Tales Volume Two

Story and Art by various

Paperback 978-1434234568 $12.95

Capstone/Stone Arch, 2012

Color, 176 pages each

OKIE DOKIE DONUTS

Story and art by Chris Eliopoulous

Hardcover 978-1603090681 $9.95

Top Shelf, 2011

Color, 48 pages

OKIE DOKIE DONUTS WHAT'S NEXT ...

The Many Adventures of Johnny Mutton

Story and art by James Promios

Paperback 978-0152166984 $6.00

Harcourt, 2001

Color, 48 pages

P.T.A. NIGHT

Story and art by Jeremy Scott

Hardcover 978-1607061632 $12.99

Image/Silverline, 2009

Color, 32 pages

P.T.A. NIGHT WHAT'S NEXT ...

Fang Fairy

Story and art by Andy J. Smith

Hardcover 978-1598898354 $21.26

Paperback 978-1598898910 $4.95

Capstone/Stone Arch, 2007

Color, 40 pages

Dear Dracula

Story by Joshua Williamson

Art by Vincente Navarette

Hardcover 978-1582409702 $7.99

Image/Silverline, 2008

Color, 48 pages

SAM & FRIENDS MYSTERIES SERIES

Story by Mary Labatt

Art by Jo Rioux

Book One: Dracula Madness

Hardcover 978-1-554534180 $16.95

Paperback 978-1-553373032 $7.95

Book Two: Lake Monster Mix-up

Hardcover 978-1-553378228 $16.95

Paperback 978-1-553373025 $7.95

Book Three: Mummy Mayhem
Hardcover 978-1-554534708 $16.95
Paperback 978-1-554534715 $7.95

Book Four: Witches' Brew
Hardcover 978-1-554534722 $16.95
Paperback 978-1-554534739 $7.95
Kids Can Press, 2009-2011
Black and white, 96 pages each

SAM & FRIENDS MYSTERIES WHAT'S NEXT ...

The 3-2-3 Detective Agency: The Disappearance of Dave Warthog
Story and art by Fiona Robinson
Paperback 978-0810970946 $9.95
Abrams/Amulet, 2009
Color, 76 pages

SKETCH MONSTERS

Story by Joshua Williamson
Art by Vincente Navarrete

Volume 1: Escape of the Scribbles
Hardcover 978-1934964699 $12.99
Oni Press, 2011
Color, 40 pages

SKETCH MONSTERS WHAT'S NEXT ...

Nina in That Makes Me Mad!
Story by Steven Kroll and Hilary Knight
Art by Hilary Knight
Hardcover 978-1935179108 $12.95
Toon Books, 2011
Color, 32 pages

Mr. Men and Little Miss series
Little Miss Sunshine: Here Comes the Sun!
Story by Michael Daedalus Kenny
Art by Victoria Maderna
Paperback 978-1421540719 $6.99

Mr. Bump: Lights, Camera, Bump!
Story by John Hardman
Art by Matthew Britton

Paperback 978-1434228024 $4.95
Viz, 2012
Color, 80 pages each

THE SQUAT BEARS SERIES

Story and art by Émile Bravo
Translation by J. Gustave McBride

Goldilocks and the Seven Squat Bears
Hardcover 978-0316083584 $14.99

The Hunger of the Seven Squat Bears
Hardcover 978-0316083614 $14.99

Beauty and the Squat Bears
Hardcover 978-0316083621 $14.99
Yen Press, 2010-2011
Color, 32 pages each

THE SQUAT BEARS SERIES WHAT'S NEXT ...

There's a Wolf at the Door: Five Classic Tales
Story by Zoë B. Alley
Art by R.W. Alley
Hardcover 978-1596432758 $19.99
Roaring Brook Press, 2008
Color, 40 pages

There's a Princess in the Palace: Five Classic Tales
Story by Zoë B. Alley
Art by R.W. Alley
Hardcover 978-1596434714 $19.99
Roaring Brook Press, 2008
Color, 40 pages

SQUISH SERIES

Story by Jennifer L. Holm
Art by Matthew Holm

No. 1: Super Amoeba
Paperback 978-0375843891 $6.99

No. 2: Brave New Pond
Paperback 978-0375843907 $6.99

No. 3: The Power of the Parasite
Paperback 978-0375843914 $6.99
Random House, 2011-12
Black and white with green, 96 pages each

SQUISH WHAT'S NEXT ...

Dragonbreath series
Story and art by Ursula Vernon

Dragonbreath
Hardcover 978-0803733633 $12.99

Attack of the Ninja Frogs
Hardcover 978-0803733657 $12.99

Curse of the Were-Wiener
Hardcover 978-0803734692 $12.99

Lair of the Bat Monster
Hardcover 978-0803735255 $12.99

No Such Thing as Ghosts
Hardcover 978-0803735279 $12.99
Penguin/Dial Books, 2009-2011
Black and white with green, 208 pages each

STINKY
Story and art by Eleanor Davis

Hardcover 978-0979923845 $12.95
Toon Books, 2008
Color, 40 pages

STINKY WHAT'S NEXT ...

Harvey Comics Classics Volume One: Casper the Friendly Ghost
Edited by Leslie Cabarga
Story and art by various creators

Paperback, 978-1593077815 $19.95
Dark Horse, 2007
Black and white with some color, 480 pages

SUPER DIAPER BABY SERIES
Story and art by Dav Pilkey

The Adventures of Super Diaper Baby
Paperback 978-0439376068 $5.99

Super Diaper Baby 2: The Invasion of the Potty Snatchers
Hardcover 978-0545175326 $9.99
Scholastic/Blue Sky Press, 2002, 2011
Black and white, 128 pages and 192 pages

SUPER DIAPER BABY
WHAT'S NEXT ...

The Adventures of Ook and Gluk: Kung-Fu Cavemen from the Future
Story and art by Dav Pilkey

Hardcover 978-0545175302 $9.99
Paperback 978-0545385770 $5.99
Scholastic/Blue Sky Press, 2010
Black and white, 176 pages

ADVENTURES IN CARTOONING SERIES

Story and art by James Sturm,
Alexis Frederick-Frost, and Andrew Arnold

Adventures in Cartooning: How to Turn Your Doodles into Comics
Paperback 978-1596433694 $12.99
First Second, 2009
Color, 112 pages

Adventures in Cartooning Activity Book
Paperback 978-1596435988 $7.99
First Second, 2010
Black and white, 80 pages

ADVENTURES IN CARTOONING WHAT'S NEXT ...

Comics to Go: 19 Stories for You to Finish and More
Story and art by Mike Herrod

Spiral-Bound 978-1934706381 $12.95
Blue Apple Books, 2008
Color, 64 pages

ADVENTURES OF RABBIT AND BEAR PAWS SERIES

Story by Christopher Meyer and Chad Solomon
Art by Chad Solomon

The Sugar Bush
Paperback 978-0973990508 $11.95

The Voyageurs
Paperback 978-0973990621 $11.95

True Hearts
Paperback 978-0973990607 $11.95

Tall Tale
Paperback 978-0973990607 $11.95

Bear Walker
Paperback 978-0973990652 $11.95
Little Spirit Bear Productions, 2006-2012
Color, 32 pages each

ADVENTURES OF RABBIT AND BEAR PAWS WHAT'S NEXT ...

Asterix series
Story by René Goscinny
Art and story by Albert Uderzo

Asterix the Gaul
Hardcover 978-0752866048 $14.95
Paperback 978-0752866055 $10.95

Asterix and the Golden Sickle
Hardcover 978-0752866123 $14.95
Paperback 978-0752866130 $10.95

Asterix and the Goths
Hardcover 978-0752866147 $14.95
Paperback 978-0752866154 $10.95

Asterix the Gladiator
Hardcover 978-0752866109 $14.95
Paperback 978-0752866116 $10.95

Asterix and the Banquet
Hardcover 978-0752866086 $14.95
Paperback 978-0752866093 $10.95

Asterix and Cleopatra
Hardcover 978-0752866062 $14.95
Paperback 978-0752866079 $10.95

Asterix and the Big Fight
Hardcover 978-0752866161 $14.95
Paperback 978-0752866178 $10.95

Asterix in Britain
Hardcover 978-0752866185 $14.95
Paperback 978-0752866192 $10.95

Asterix and the Normans
Hardcover 978-0752866222 $14.95
Paperback 978-0752866239 $10.95

Asterix the Legionary
Hardcover 978-0752866208 $14.95
Paperback 978-0752866215 $10.95

Asterix and the Chieftain's Shield
Hardcover 978-0752866246 $14.95
Paperback 978-0752866253 $10.95

Asterix and the Olympic Games
Hardcover 978-0752866260 $14.95
Paperback 978-0752866277 $10.95

Asterix and the Cauldron
Hardcover 978-0752866284 $14.95
Paperback 978-0752866291 $10.95

Asterix in Spain
Hardcover 978-0752866307 $14.95
Paperback 978-0752866314 $10.95

Asterix and the Roman Agent
Hardcover 978-0752866321 $14.95
Paperback 978-0752866338 $10.95

Asterix in Switzerland
Hardcover 978-0752866345 $14.95
Paperback 978-0752866352 $10.95

Asterix: The Mansions of the Gods
Hardcover 978-0752866383 $14.95
Paperback 978-0752866390 $10.95

Asterix and the Laurel Wreath
Hardcover 978-0752866369 $14.95
Paperback 978-0752866376 $10.95

Asterix and the Soothsayer
Hardcover 978-0752866413 $14.95
Paperback 978-0752866420 $10.95

Asterix in Corsica
Hardcover 978-0752866437 $14.95
Paperback 978-0752866444 $10.95

Asterix and Caesar's Gift
Hardcover 978-0752866451 $14.95
Paperback 978-0752866468 $10.95

Asterix and the Great Crossing
Hardcover 978-0752866475 $14.95
Paperback 978-0752866482 $10.95

Obelix and Co.
Hardcover 978-0752866512 $14.95
Paperback 978-0752866529 $10.95

Asterix in Belgium
Hardcover 978-0752866499 $14.95
Paperback 978-0752866505 $10.95

Asterix and the Great Divide
Hardcover 978-0752847122 $14.95
Paperback 978-0752847733 $10.95

Asterix and the Black Gold
Hardcover 978-0752847139 $14.95
Paperback 978-0752847740 $10.95

Asterix and Son
Hardcover 978-0752847146 $14.95
Paperback 978-0752847146 $10.95

Asterix and the Magic Carpet
Hardcover 978-0752847153 $14.95
Paperback 978-0752847153 $10.95

Asterix and the Secret Weapon
Hardcover 978-0752847160 $14.95
Paperback 978-0752847771 $10.95

Asterix and Obelix All at Sea
Hardcover 978-0752847177 $14.95
Paperback 978-0752847788 $10.95

Asterix and the Actress
Hardcover 978-0752846576 $14.95
Paperback 978-0752846583 $10.95

Asterix and the Class Act
Hardcover 978-0752860688 $14.95
Paperback 978-0752866406 $10.95

Asterix and the Falling Sky
Hardcover 978-0320075698 $14.95
Paperback 978-0752875484 $10.95

Asterix and Obelix's Birthday
Hardcover 978-1444000276 $14.95
Paperback 978-1444000955 $10.95
Orion, 2004-2011
Color, 48-56 pages

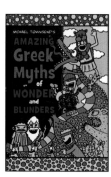

AMAZING GREEK MYTHS OF WONDERS AND BLUNDERS

Story and art by Michael Townsend
Hardcover 978-0803733084 $14.99
Dial Books for Young Readers, 2010
Color, 160 pages

AMAZING GREEK MYTHS OF WONDERS AND BLUNDERS WHAT'S NEXT ...

Pirate Penguin vs. Ninja Chicken: Troublems with Frenemies
Story and art by Ray Friesen
Hardcover 978-1603090711 $9.95
Top Shelf, 2011
Color, 96 pages

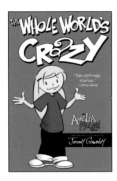

AMELIA RULES SERIES

Story and art by Jimmy Gownley

Volume 1: The Whole World's Crazy
Hardcover 978-1442445383 $19.99
Paperback 978-1416986041 $10.99
Volume 2: What Makes You Happy
Hardcover 978-1442445390 $19.99
Paperback 978-1416986058 $10.99
Volume 3: Superheroes
Hardcover 978-1442445406 $19.99
Paperback 978-1416986065 $10.99
Volume 4: When the Past Is a Present
Hardcover 978-1442445413 $19.99
Paperback 978-1416986072 $10.99
Volume 5: The Tweenage Guide to Not Being Unpopular
Hardcover 978-1416986102 $18.99
Paperback 978-1416986089 $10.99
Volume 6: True Things (Adults Don't Want Kids to Know)
Hardcover 978-1416986119 $18.99
Paperback 978-1416986096 $10.99
Volume 7: The Meaning of Life ... And Other Stuff
Hardcover 978-1416986133 $19.99
Paperback 978-1416986126 $10.99
Simon & Schuster/Atheneum, 2003-2011
Color, 160-192 pages

AMELIA RULES WHAT'S NEXT ...

Oddly Normal series
Story and art by Otis Frampton

Vol. 1: Oddly Normal
Paperback 978-0977788309 $11.95
Vol. 2: Family Reunion
Paperback 978-0977788392 $11.95
SLG Publishing, 2006-2007
Color, 112-128 pages

CHICAGOLAND DETECTIVE AGENCY SERIES

Story by Trina Robbins
Art by Tyler Page
Lettering by Zack Giallongo

#1: The Drained Brains Caper
Paperback 978-0761356356 $6.95
#2: The Maltese Mummy
Paperback 978-0761356363 $6.95
#3: Night of the Living Dogs
Paperback 978-0761356370 $6.95
Lerner/Graphic Universe, 2010-2011
Black and white, 64 pages each

CHICAGOLAND DETECTIVE AGENCY WHAT'S NEXT ...

Scared to Death series
Story by Virginie Van Holme
Art by Mauricet
Color by Laurent Carpentier
Translation by Luke Spear

#1: The Vampire from the Marshes
Paperback 978-1905460472 $11.95
#2: Malevolence and Mandrake
Paperback 978-1905460779 $11.95
Cinebook, 2008-2009
Color, 48 pages each

Leave It to Chance series
Story by James Robinson
Art by Paul Smith

Shaman's Rain
Hardcover 978-1582402536 out of print
Trick or Treat
Hardcover 978-1582402789 $12.95
Monster Madness
Hardcover 978-1582402987 $12.95
Image, 2002-2003
Color, 112 pages each

CHI'S SWEET HOME SERIES
Story and art by Konami Kanata
Translation by Ed Chavez

Volume 1
Paperback 978-1934287811 $13.95
Volume 2
Paperback 978-1934287859 $13.95
Volume 3
Paperback 978-1934287910 $13.95
Volume 4
Paperback 978-1934287965 $13.95
Volume 5
Paperback 978-1934287132 $13.95
Volume 6
Paperback 978-1934287148 $13.95
Volume 7
Paperback 978-1935654216 $13.95
Volume 8
Paperback 978-1935654353 $13.95
Vertical, 2010-2012
Color, 152-168 pages

CHI'S SWEET HOME WHAT'S NEXT ...
One Fine Day series
Story and art by Sirial
Translation by JuYoun Lee

Volume 1
Paperback 978-0759530560 $10.99
Volume 2
Paperback 978-0759530577 $10.99
Volume 3
Paperback 978-0316097611 $10.99
Yen Press, 2010
Black and white, 160-176 pages

COWA!
Story and art by Akira Toriyama
Translation by Alexander O. Smith
Paperback 978-1421518053 $7.99
Viz, 2008
Black and white with 16-page color insert,
208 pages

COWA! WHAT'S NEXT ...
Beet the Vandel Buster series
Story by Riku Sanjo
Art by Koji Inada

Volume 1
Paperback 978-1591166900 $7.99
Volume 2
Paperback 978-1591166917 $7.99
Volume 3
Paperback 978-1591166931 $7.99
Volume 4
Paperback 978-1591167501 $7.99
Volume 5
Paperback 978-1591168065 $7.99
Volume 6
Paperback 978-1591168713 $7.99
Volume 7
Paperback 978-1421500768 $7.99
Volume 8
Paperback 978-1421501475 $7.99
Volume 9
Paperback 978-1421502700 $7.99
Volume 10
Paperback 978-1421507712 $7.99
Volume 11
Paperback 978-1421511573 $7.99
Volume 12
Paperback 978-1421514062 $7.99
Viz, 2004-2007
Black and white, 184-216 pages

ELEPHANTS NEVER FORGET SERIES
Story and art by Bill Slavin

#1: Big City Otto
Hardcover 978-0545175326 $16.95
Paperback 978-0545175326 $7.95
Kids Can Press, 2011
Color, 80 pages

ELEPHANTS NEVER FORGET WHAT'S NEXT ...

Spiral-Bound
Story and art by Aaron Renier
Paperback 978-1891830501 $14.95
Top Shelf, 2005
Black and white, 144 pages

The Muppet Show series
Story by Roger Langridge
Art by Roger Langridge and Amy Mebberson

Meet the Muppets
Paperback 978-1934506851 $9.99

Family Reunion
Paperback 978-1608865888 $9.99

The Treasure of Peg-Leg Wilson
Paperback 978-1608865048 $9.99

Muppet Mash
Paperback 978-1608866113 $9.99
Boom! Studios, 2009-2011
Color, 112-128 pages

THE ELSEWHERE CHRONICLES SERIES
Story by Nykko
Art by Bannister
Colors by Corentin Jaffré

Book One: The Shadow Door
Paperback 978-0761339632 $6.95
Book Two: The Shadow Spies
Paperback 978-0761339649 $6.95
Book Three: The Master of Shadows
Paperback 978-0761347446 $6.95
Book Four: The Calling
Paperback 978-0761360698 $6.95
Book Five: The Parting
Paperback 978-0761375241 $6.95
Lerner/Graphic Universe, 2009-2011
Color, 48 pages each

THE ELSEWHERE CHRONICLES WHAT'S NEXT ...

Vermonia series
Story and art by Yoyo

#1 Quest for the Silver Tiger
Paperback 978-0763645540 $7.99
#2 Call of the Winged Panther
Paperback 978-0763647384 $7.99
#3 Release of the Red Phoenix
Paperback 978-0763647858 $7.99
#4 The Rukan Prophecy
Paperback 978-0763649500 $7.99
#5 The Warriors' Trial
Paperback 978-0763656102 $7.99
#6 To the Pillar of Wind
Paperback 978-0763659172 $7.99
Candlewick, 2009-2012
Black and white, 208 pages each

G-MAN SERIES

Story and art by Chris Giarrusso

#1: Learning to Fly
Paperback 978-1607060871 $9.99

#2: Cape Crisis
Paperback 978-1607062714 $9.99
Image, 2009-2010
Color, 96 pages and 128 pages

G-MAN WHAT'S NEXT ...

Franklin Richards series
Story by Chris Eliopoulos with Marc Sumarek
Art by Chris Eliopoulos

Franklin Richards: Son of a Genius Ultimate Collection Book 1
Paperback 978-0785149248 $19.99

Franklin Richards: Son of a Genius Ultimate Collection Book 2
Paperback 978-0785149248 $19.99
Marvel, 2010
Color, 184 pages and 216 pages

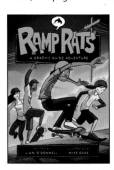

GRAPHIC GUIDE ADVENTURES SERIES

Story by Liam O'Donnell
Art by Mike Deas

Wild Ride
Paperback 978-1551437569 $9.95
Ramp Rats
Paperback 978-1551438801 $9.95
Soccer Sabotage
Paperback 978-1551438849 $9.95
Media Meltdown
Paperback 978-1554690657 $9.95
Food Fight
Paperback 978-1554690671 $9.95
Power Play
Paperback 978-1554690695 $9.95
Orca Books, 2007-2011
Color, 64 pages each

GRAPHIC GUIDE ADVENTURES WHAT'S NEXT ...

Howtoons: The Possibilities are Endless!
Story by Saul Griffith and Joost Bonsen
Art by Nick Dragotta
Paperback 978-0060761585 out of print
HarperCollins, 2007
Color, 112 pages

HAPPY HAPPY CLOVER SERIES

Story and art by Sayuri Tatsuyama
Translation by Kaori Inoue

Volume 1
Paperback 978-1421526560 $7.99
Volume 2
Paperback 978-1421526577 $7.99
Volume 3
Paperback 978-1421526584 $7.99
Volume 4
Paperback 978-1421527352 $7.99
Volume 5
Paperback 978-1421527369 $7.99
Viz, 2009-2010
Black and white, 192 pages each

HAPPY HAPPY CLOVER WHAT'S NEXT ...

Fairy Idol Kanon series
Story and art by Mera Hakamada
Translation by M. Kirie Hayashi

Volume 1
Paperback 978-1897376898 $7.99
Volume 2
Paperback 978-1897376904 $7.99
Volume 3
Paperback 978-1897376911 $7.99
Volume 4
Paperback 978-1897376928 $7.99
Udon Entertainment, 2009-2010
Black and white, 200 pages each

KNIGHTS OF THE LUNCH TABLE SERIES

Story and art by Frank Cammuso

The Dodgeball Chronicles
Paperback 978-0439903226 $9.99
The Dragon Players
Paperback 978-0439903233 $9.99
The Battling Bands
Paperback 978-0439903189 $10.99
Scholastic/Graphix, 2008-2011
Color, 128-144 pages

KNIGHTS OF THE LUNCH TABLE WHAT'S NEXT ...

World of Quest series
Story and art by Jason T. Kruse

Volume 1
Paperback 978-0759524026 $9.99
Volume 2
Paperback 978-0759528895 $9.99
Yen Press, 2007-2008
Color, 144 pages each

LITTLE VAMPIRE

Story and art by Joann Sfar
Paperback 978-1596432338 $13.99
First Second, 2008
Color, 96 pages

LITTLE VAMPIRE WHAT'S NEXT ...

Scary Godmother
Story and art by Jill Thompson
Hardcover 978-1595825896 $24.99
Dark Horse, 2010
Color, 192 pages

MISSILE MOUSE SERIES

Story and art by Jake Parker

Missile Mouse: The Star Crusher
Hardcover 978-0545117142 $21.99
Paperback 978-0545117159 $10.99
Missile Mouse: Rescue on Tankium3
Hardcover 978-0545117166 $21.99
Paperback 978-0545117173 $10.99
Scholastic/Graphix, 2009-2010
Color, 168 pages and 176 pages

MISSILE MOUSE WHAT'S NEXT ...

Star Wars Adventures series
Han Solo and the Hollow Moon of Khorya
Story by Jeremy Barlow

Art by Rick Lacy, Matthew Loux, and Michael Atiyeh
Paperback 978-1595821980 $7.95
Princess Leia and the Royal Ransom
Story by Jeremy Barlow
Art by Carlo Soriano
Paperback 978-1595821478 $7.95
**Luke Skywalker and the Treasure of the
Dragonsnakes**
Story by Tom Taylor
Art by Daxiong
Paperback 978-1595823472 $7.95
The Will of Darth Vader
Story by Tom Taylor
Art by Brian Koschak, Dan Parsons,
and Michael Wiggam
Paperback 978-1595824356 $7.95
Boba Fett and the Ship of Fear
Story by Jeremy Barlow
Art by Daxiong
Paperback 978-1595824363 $7.99
Chewbacca and the Slavers of the Shadowlands
Story by Chris Cerasi
Art by Jennifer Mayer
Paperback 978-1595827647 $7.99
Dark Horse, 2009-2011
Color, 72-80 pages

NINJA BASEBALL KYUMA SERIES

Story and art by Shunshin Maeda

Volume 1
Paperback 978-1897376867 $7.99
Volume 2
Paperback 978-1897376874 $7.99
Volume 3
Paperback 978-1897376881 $7.99
Udon, 2009-2010
Black and white, 200 pages each

NINJA BASEBALL KYUMA WHAT'S NEXT ...

Whistle series
Story and art by Daisuke Higuchi

Volume 1
Paperback 978-1591166856 $7.99
Volume 2
Paperback 978-1591166863 $7.99
Volume 3
Paperback 978-1591166924 $7.99
Volume 4
Paperback 978-1591167273 $7.99
Volume 5
Paperback 978-1591167891 $7.99
Volume 6
Paperback 978-1591168362 $7.99
Volume 7
Paperback 978-1591169734 $7.99
Volume 8
Paperback 978-1421500683 $7.99
Volume 9
Paperback 978-1421502069 $7.99
Volume 10
Paperback 978-1421503400 $7.99
Volume 11
Paperback 978-1421506852 $7.99
Volume 12
Paperback 978-1421506869 $7.99
Volume 13
Paperback 978-1421506876 $7.99
Volume 14
Paperback 978-1421506883 $7.99
Volume 15
Paperback 978-1421506890 $7.99
Volume 16
Paperback 978-1421511078 $7.99
Volume 17
Paperback 978-1421511085 $7.99
Volume 18
Paperback 978-1421511092 $7.99
Volume 19
Paperback 978-1421511108 $7.99
Volume 20
Paperback 978-1421511115 $7.99
Volume 21
Paperback 978-1421516561 $7.99
Volume 22
Paperback 978-1421524450 $7.99
Volume 23
Paperback 978-1421524467 $7.99

Volume 24
Paperback 978-1421524474 $9.99
Viz, 2004-2010
Black and white, 200-208 pages

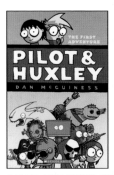

PILOT AND HUXLEY SERIES
Story and art by Dan McGuiness

The First Adventure
Paperback 978-0545265041 $8.99
The Next Adventure
Paperback 978-0545268455 $8.99
Scholastic/Graphix, 2011
Color, 64 pages each

PILOT AND HUXLEY WHAT'S NEXT ...
Pinky and Stinky
Story and art by James Kochalka
Paperback 978-0759524026 $15
Top Shelf, 2002
Black and white, 208 pages
Dalen and Gole: Scandal in Port Angus
Story and art by Mike Deas
Paperback 978-1554698004 $9.95
Orca Books, 2011
Color, 128 pages

RAPUNZEL'S REVENGE SERIES
Story by Shannon and Dean Hale
Art by Nathan Hale

Rapunzel's Revenge
Hardcover 978-1599900704 $18.99
Paperback 978-1599902883 $15.99
Calamity Jack
Hardcover 978-1599900766 $19.99
Paperback 978-1599903736 $14.99
Bloomsbury, 2008-2010
Color, 144 pages each

RAPUNZEL'S REVENGE SERIES WHAT'S NEXT ...
Wonderland
Story by Tommy Kovac
Art by Sonny Liew
Hardcover 978-1423104513 $19.99
Disney Press, 2008
Color, 160 pages

ROBOT CITY ADVENTURES SERIES
Story and art by Paul Collicutt

#1: City in Peril!
Paperback 978-0763641207 $8.99
#2: Rust Attack!
Paperback 978-0763645946 $8.99
#3: The Indestructible Metal Men
Paperback 978-0763650148 $8.99
#4: Murder on the Robot City Express
Paperback 978-0763650155 $8.99
Candlewick/Templar, 2009-2010
Color, 48 pages each

ROBOT CITY ADVENTURES SERIES WHAT'S NEXT ...
Joey Fly, Private Eye series
Story by Aaron Reynolds
Art by Neil Numberman

Volume 1: Creepy Crawly Crime
Hardcover 978-0805082425 $16.99
Paperback 978-0805087864 $9.99
Volume 2: Big Hairy Drama
Hardcover 978-0805082432 $16.99

Paperback 978-0805091106 $9.99
Henry Holt Books for Young Readers, 2009-2010
Color, 96-128 pages

ROBOT DREAMS

Story and art by Sarah Varon

Paperback 978-1596431089 $16.95
First Second, 2007
Color, 208 pages

ROBOT DREAMS WHAT'S NEXT ...

The Clouds Above
Story and art by Jordan Crane

Hardcover 978-1560976271 $18.95
Paperback 978-1560979098 $16.99
Fantagraphics, 2005
Color, 224 pages

Bake Sale
Story and art by Sara Varon

Hardcover 978-1596437401 $19.99
Paperback 978-1596434196 $16.99
First Second, 2011
Color, 160 pages

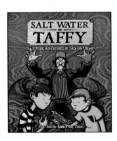

SALT WATER TAFFY: THE SEASIDE ADVENTURES OF JACK AND BENNY SERIES

Story and art by Matthew Loux

#1: The Legend of Old Salty
Paperback 978-1932664942 $5.95
#2: A Climb up Mt. Barnabas
Paperback 978-1934964033 $5.95
#3: The Truth about Dr. True
Paperback 978-1934964040 $5.95
#4: Caldera's Revenge, Part I
Paperback 978-1934964620 $5.95
#5: Caldera's Revenge, Part II
Paperback 978-1934964637 $5.95
Oni Press, 2008-2011
Black and white, 72-96 pages

SALT WATER TAFFY: THE SEASIDE ADVENTURES OF JACK AND BENNY SERIES WHAT'S NEXT ...

Shadow Rock
Story and art by Jeremy Love and Robert Love

Paperback 978-1593073473 $9.95
Dark Horse, 2006
Color, 80 pages

SARDINE IN OUTER SPACE SERIES

Story by Emmanuel Guibert
Art by Joann Sfar (*Books One to Four*)

Story and art by Emmanuel Guibert
(*Books Five and Six*)

Book One
Paperback 978-1596431263 $14.95
Book Two
Paperback 978-1596431270 $14.95
Book Three
Paperback 978-1596431288 $14.95
Book Four
Paperback 978-1596431294 $14.95
Book Five
Paperback 978-0545175326 $14.95

Book Six
Paperback 978-0545175326 $14.95
First Second, 2006-2008
Color, 96-128 pages

SARDINE IN OUTER SPACE WHAT'S NEXT ...

Kaput and Zosky
Story and art by Lewis Trondheim
Paperback 978-1596431324 $13.95
First Second, 2008
Color, 80 pages

THE SECRET SCIENCE ALLIANCE AND THE COPYCAT CROOK

Story and art by Eleanor Davis
Hardcover 978-1599901428 $18.99
Paperback 978-1599903965 $11.99
Bloomsbury, 2009
Color, 160 pages

THE SECRET SCIENCE ALLIANCE AND THE COPYCAT CROOK WHAT'S NEXT ...

Mal and Chad series
Story and art by Stephen McCranie

The Biggest, Bestest Time Ever!
Paperback 978-0399252211 $9.99
Food Fight!
Paperback 978-0399256578 $9.99
Philomel, 2011-2012
Color, 224 pages each

SIDEKICKS

Story and art by Dan Santat
Hardcover 978-0439298117 $24.99
Paperback 978-0439298193 $12.99
Scholastic/Arthur Levine Books, 2011
Color, 224 pages

SIDEKICKS WHAT'S NEXT ...

Scratch9
Story by Rob M. Worley
Art by Jason T. Kruse and Mike Kunkel

Volume 1: The Pet Project
Paperback 978-1936340538 $9.95
Ape Entertainment, 2011
Color, 100 pages

THE SMURFS SERIES

Story by Yvan Delporte, Gos, and Peyo
Art by Peyo and Gos

The Purple Smurfs
Hardcover 978-1597072069 $10.99
Paperback 978-1597072076 $5.99

The Smurfs and the Magic Flute
Hardcover 978-1597072083 $10.99
Paperback 978-1597072096 $5.99

The Smurf King
Hardcover 978-1597072243 $10.99
Paperback 978-1597072250 $5.99

The Smurfette
Hardcover 978-1561632373 $10.99
Paperback 978-1597072366 $5.99

The Smurfs and the Egg
Hardcover 978-1561632472 $10.99
Paperback 978-1597072465 $5.99

The Smurfs and the Howlibird
Hardcover 978-1561632618 $10.99
Paperback 978-1597072601 $5.99

The Astro Smurf
Hardcover 978-1597072519 $10.99
Paperback 978-1597072502 $5.99

The Smurf Apprentice
Hardcover 978-1597072809 $10.99
Paperback 978-1597072793 $5.99

Gargamel and the Smurfs
Hardcover 978-1597072908 $10.99
Paperback 978-1597072892 $5.99

The Return of Smurfette
Hardcover 978-1597072939 $10.99
Paperback 978-1597072922 $5.99

The Smurf Olympics
Hardcover 978-1597073028 $10.99
Paperback 978-1597073011 $5.99
Papercutz, 2010-2011
Color, 56-64 pages

THE SMURFS WHAT'S NEXT ...

Moomin series
Story and art by Tove Jansson and Lars Jansson
(Book Six)

Book One
Hardcover 978-1894937801 $19.95

Book Two
Hardcover 978-1897299197 $19.95

Book Three
Hardcover 978-1897299555 $19.95

Book Four
Hardcover 978-1897299784 $19.95

Book Five
Hardcover 978-1897299944 $19.95

Book Six
Hardcover 978-1770460423 $19.95
Drawn and Quarterly, 2006-2011
Black and white, 88-128 pages

THREE THIEVES SERIES
Story and art by Scott Chantler

Tower of Treasure
Hardcover 978-1554534142 $17.95
Paperback 978-1554534159 $8.95

The Sign of the Black Rock
Hardcover 978-1554534166 $17.95
Paperback 978-1554534173 $8.95
Kids Can Press, 2010-2011
Color, 112 pages each

THREE THIEVES WHAT'S NEXT ...

Alison Dare series
Story by J. Torres
Art by J. Bone

Little Miss Adventures
Paperback 978-0887769344 $10.95

The Heart of the Maiden
Paperback 978-0887769351 $10.95
Tundra, 2010
Black and white, 96-104 pages

TINY TYRANT SERIES
Story by Lewis Trondheim
Art by Fabrice Parme
Translation by Alexis Siegel

Volume 1: The Ethelbertosaurus
Paperback 978-1596435100 $9.95
Volume 2: The Lucky Winner
Hardcover 978-1596435230 $9.99
First Second, 2007
Color, 64 pages each

TINY TYRANT WHAT'S NEXT ...

Princess at Midnight
Story and art by Andi Watson

Paperback 978-1582409283 $5.99
Image, 2008
Black and white, 64 pages

TO DANCE: A BALLERINA'S GRAPHIC NOVEL

Story by Siena Cherson Siegel
Art by Mark Siegel

Hardcover 978-0689867477 $17.95
Paperback 978-1416926870 $9.99
Simon & Schuster/Atheneum, 2006
Color, 64 pages

TO DANCE: A BALLERINA'S GRAPHIC NOVEL WHAT'S NEXT ...

Lily Renée, Escape Artist: From Holocaust Survivor to Comic Book Pioneer
Story by Trina Robbins
Art by Anne Timmons and Mo Oh

Hardcover 978-0761360100 $29.27
Paperback 978-0761381143 $7.95
Lerner/Graphic Universe, 2011
Color, 96 pages

WIZARD OF OZ SERIES

Story by L. Frank Baum
Adapted by Eric Shanower
Art by Skottie Young
Colors by Jean-Francis Beaulieu

The Wonderful Wizard of Oz
Hardcover 978-0785129219 $29.99
Paperback 978-0785145905 $19.99
The Marvelous Land of Oz
Hardcover 978-078514028-3 $29.99
Paperback 978-0785140870 $19.99
Ozma of Oz
Hardcover 978-0785142478 $29.99
Marvel, 2009-2011
Color, 192-200 pages

WIZARD OF OZ SERIES WHAT'S NEXT ...

Little Adventures in Oz series
Story and art by Eric Shanower

Volume 1
Paperback 978-1600105890 $9.99
Volume 2
Paperback 978-1600106781 $9.99
IDW, 2010
Color, 136 pages each
Baron: the Cat Returns
Story and art by Aoi Hiiragi

Paperback 978-1591169567 out of print
Viz, 2005
Black and white, 224 pages

YOTSUBA&! SERIES

Story and art by Kiyohiko Azuma
Translation by Amy Forsyth (Vols. 1, 4-9);
Stephen Paul (Vols. 2-3)

Volume 1
Paperback 978-0316073875 $10.99
Volume 2
Paperback 978-0316073899 $10.99
Volume 3
Paperback 978-0316073905 $10.99
Volume 4
Paperback 978-0316073912 $10.99
Volume 5
Paperback 978-0316073929 $10.99
Volume 6
Paperback 978-0316073240 $10.99
Volume 7
Paperback 978-0316073257 $10.99
Volume 8
Paperback 978-0316073271 $10.99
Volume 9
Paperback 978-0316126793 $10.99
Volume 10
Paperback 978-0316190336 $10.99
Yen Press, 2009-2011
Black and white, 192-224 pages

YOTSUBA&! WHAT'S NEXT ...

Little Lulu series
Story and art by John Stanley and Irving Tripp

Vol. 1: My Dinner with Lulu
Paperback 978-1593073183 $9.95
Vol. 2: Sunday Afternoon
Paperback 978-1593073459 $9.95
Vol. 3: In the Doghouse
Paperback 978-1593073466 $9.95
Vol. 4: Lulu Goes Shopping

Paperback 978-1593072704 $9.95
Vol. 5: Lulu Takes a Trip
Paperback 978-1593073176 $9.95
Vol. 6: Letters to Santa
Paperback 978-1593073862 $9.95
Vol. 7: Lulu's Umbrella Service
Paperback 978-1593073992 $9.95
Vol. 8: Late for School
Paperback 978-1593074531 $9.95
Vol. 9: Lucky Lulu
Paperback 978-1593074715 $9.95
Vol. 10: All Dressed Up
Paperback 978-1593075347 $9.95
Vol. 11: April Fools
Paperback 978-1593075576 $9.95
Vol. 12: Leave It to Lulu
Paperback 978-1593076207 $9.95
Vol. 13: Too Much Fun
Paperback 978-1593076214 $9.95
Vol. 14: Queen Lulu
Paperback 978-1593076832 $9.95
Vol. 15: The Explorers
Paperback 978-1593076849 $10.95
Vol. 16: A Handy Kid
Paperback 978-1593076856 $10.95
Vol. 17: The Valentine
Paperback 978-1593076863 $10.95
Vol. 18: The Expert
Paperback 978-1593076870 $10.95
Vol. 19: The Alamo and Other Stories
Paperback 978-1595822932 $14.95
Vol. 20: The Bawlplayers and Other Stories
Paperback 978-1595823649 $14.95
Vol. 21: Miss Feeny's Folly and Other Stories
Paperback 978-1595823656 $14.95
Vol. 22: The Big Dipper Club and Other Stories
Paperback 978-1595824202 $14.99
Vol. 23: The Bogey Snowman and Other Stories
Paperback 978-1595824745 $14.99
Vol. 24: The Space Dolly and Other Stories
Paperback 978-1595824752 $14.99
**Vol. 25: The Burglar-Proof Clubhouse
and Other Stories**
Paperback 978-1595825391 $14.99
Vol. 26: The Feud and Other Stories
Paperback 978-1595826329 $14.99
Vol. 27: The Treasure Map and Other Stories
Paperback 978-1595826336 $14.99
Vol. 28: The Prize Winner and Other Stories

Paperback 978-1595827319 $14.99
Vol. 29: The Cranky Giant and Other Stories
Paperback 978-1595827326 $14.99
Dark Horse, 2005-2011
Black and white (Vol. 1-18), Color (Vol. 19-29),
200-240 pages

ZITA THE SPACEGIRL SERIES

Story and art by Ben Hatke

Book One: Far from Home
Hardcover 978-1596436954 $17.99
Paperback 978-1596434462 $10.99
First Second, 2011
Color, 192 pages

ZITA THE SPACEGIRL
WHAT'S NEXT ...

Korgi series
Story and art by Christian Slade
Book 1: Sprouting Wings
Paperback 978-1891830907 $10
Book 2: The Cosmic Collector
Paperback 978-1603090100 $10
Book 3: A Hollow Beginning
Paperback 978-1603090629 $10
Top Shelf, 2007-2011
Black and white, 80-96 pages
Swans in Space series
Story and art by Lun Lun Yamamoto
Translation by M. Kirie Hayashi

Volume 1
Paperback 978-1897376935 $8.99
Volume 2
Paperback 978-1897376942 $8.99
Volume 3
Paperback 978-1897376959 $8.99
Udon Entertainment, 2009-2010
Color, 128-160 pages

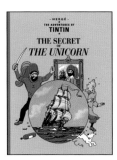

THE ADVENTURES OF TINTIN SERIES

Story and art by Hergé
Translation by Leslie Lonsdale-Cooper and Michael Turner

Tintin in America
Paperback 978-0316358521 $10.99

Cigars of the Pharaoh
Paperback 978-0316358361 $10.99

The Blue Lotus
Paperback 978-0316358569 $10.99

The Broken Ear
Paperback 978-0316358507 $10.99

The Black Island
Paperback 978-0316358354 $10.99

King Ottokar's Sceptre
Paperback 978-0316358316 $10.99

The Crab with the Golden Claws
Paperback 978-0439376068 $10.99

The Shooting Star
Paperback 978-0316358514 $10.99

The Secret of the Unicorn
Paperback 978-0316358323 $10.99

Red Rackham's Treasure
Paperback 978-0316358347 $10.99

The Seven Crystal Balls
Paperback 978-0316358408 $10.99

Prisoners of the Sun
Paperback 978-0316358439 $10.99

Land of Black Gold
Paperback 978-0316358446 $10.99

Destination Moon
Paperback 978-0316358453 $10.99

Explorers on the Moon
Paperback 978-0316358460 $10.99

The Calculus Affair
Paperback 978-0316358477 $10.99

The Red Sea Sharks
Paperback 978-0316358484 $10.99

Tintin in Tibet
Paperback 978-0316358392 $10.99

The Castafiore Emerald
Paperback 978-0316358422 $10.99

Flight 714 to Sydney
Paperback 978-0316358378 $10.99

Tintin and the Picaros
Paperback 978-0316358491 $10.99
Little, Brown, 1945-1976
Color, 64 pages each

THE ADVENTURES OF TINTIN WHAT'S NEXT ...

City of Spies
Story by Susan Kim and Laurence Klavan
Art by Pascal Dizin
Paperback 978-1596432628 $16.99
First Second, 2010
Color, 176 pages

Alex Rider Adventures series
Original stories by Anthony Horowitz
Adapted by Antony Johnston
Art by Kanako and Yuzuru

Stormbreaker
Paperback 978-0399246333 $16.99

Point Blank
Paperback 978-0399250262 $16.99

Skeleton Key
Paperback 978-0399254185 $16.99
Philomel, 2006-2009
Color, 128-144 pages

AMELIA EARHART: THIS BROAD OCEAN

Story by Sarah Stewart Taylor
Art by Ben Towle
Introduction by Eileen Collins
Hardcover 978-1423113379 $17.99
Disney/Hyperion, 2010
Black and white with blue, 80 pages

AMELIA EARHART: THIS BROAD OCEAN
WHAT'S NEXT ...
No Girls Allowed: Tales of Daring Women Dressed as Men for Love, Freedom and Adventure
Story by Susan Hughes
Art by Willow Dawson

Hardcover 978-1554531776 $16.95
Paperback 978-1554531783 $8.95
Kids Can Press, 2008
Black and white, 80 pages

The Wright Brothers
Story by Lewis Helfand
Art by Sankha Banerjee

Paperback 978-9380028460 $9.99
Campfire, 2011
Color, 72 pages

AMULET SERIES
Story and art by Kazu Kibuishi
Colors by Jason Caffoe

Book One: The Stonekeeper
Paperback 978-0439846813 $10.99
Book Two: The Stonekeeper's Curse
Hardcover 978-0439846838 $10.99
Book Three: The Cloud Searchers
Hardcover 978-0545208857 $10.99
Book Four: The Last Council
Hardcover 978-0545208871 $10.99
Scholastic/Graphix, 2008-2011
Color, 192-224 pages

AMULET WHAT'S NEXT ...

Ghostopolis
Story and art by Doug TenNapel

Hardcover 978-0545210270 $24.99
Paperback 978-0545210287 $12.99
Scholastic/Graphix, 2010
Color, 272 pages

ARCHIE: FRESHMAN YEAR SERIES
Story by Batton Lash
Art by Bill Galvan and Bob Smith

The High School Chronicles
Paperback 978-1879794405 $10.95
The Missing Chapters
Paperback 978-1879794719 $9.95
Archie Comics, 2009-2011
Color, 112 pages and 128 pages

ARCHIE: FRESHMAN YEAR
WHAT'S NEXT ...

Itazura na Kiss series
Story and art by Kaoru Tada

Volume 1
Paperback 978-1569701317 $16.95
Volume 2
Paperback 978-1569701362 $16.95
Volume 3
Paperback 978-1569701713 $16.95
Volume 4
Paperback 978-1569701911 $16.95
Volume 5
Paperback 978-1569701928 $16.95
Volume 6
Paperback 978-1569701973 $16.95
Volume 7
Paperback 978-1569702284 $16.95
Digital Manga Publishing, 2009-2011
Black and white, 300-376 pages

THE ARRIVAL

Story and art by Shaun Tan

Hardcover 978-0439895293 $19.99
Scholastic/Arthur Levine Books, 2006
Black and white with sepia, 128 pages

THE ARRIVAL WHAT'S NEXT ...

Around the World: Three Remarkable Journeys
Story and art by Matt Phelan

Hardcover 978-0763636197 $24.99
Candlewick, 2011
Color, 240 pages

ASTRONAUT ACADEMY: ZERO GRAVITY

Story and art by Dave Roman

Hardcover 978-1596437562 $16.99
Paperback 978-1596436206 $9.99
First Second, 2011
Black and white, 192 pages

ASTRONAUT ACADEMY: ZERO GRAVITY WHAT'S NEXT ...

Hollow Fields Omnibus
Story and art by Madeleine Rosca

Paperback 978-1934876725 $14.99
Seven Seas, 2009
Black and white, 544 pages

BAD ISLAND

Story and art by Doug TenNapel
Colors by Katherine Garner and Josh Kenfield

Hardcover 978-0545314794 $24.99
Paperback, 978-0545314800 $10.99
Scholastic/Graphix, 2011
Color, 224 pages

BAD ISLAND WHAT'S NEXT ...

Into the Volcano
Story and art by Don Wood

Hardcover 978-0439726719 $18.99
Scholastic/Blue Sky Press, 2008
Color, 176 pages

BONE SERIES

Story and art by Jeff Smith
Colors by Steve Hamaker

#1: Out from Boneville
Hardcover 978-0439706230 $18.99
Paperback 978-0439706407 $9.99

#2: The Great Cow Race
Hardcover 978-0439706247 $18.99
Paperback 978-0439706391 $9.99

#3: Eyes of the Storm
Hardcover 978-0439706254 $18.99

Paperback 978-0439706384 $9.99

#4: The Dragonslayer
Hardcover 978-0439706261 $18.99
Paperback 978-0439706377 $9.99

#5: Rock Jaw, Master of the Eastern Border
Hardcover 978-0439706278 $18.99
Paperback 978-0439706360 $9.99

#6: Old Man's Cave
Hardcover 978-0439706285 $18.99
Paperback 978-04397062853 $9.99

#7: Ghost Circles
Hardcover 978-0439706292 $19.99
Paperback 978-0439706346 $9.99

#8: Treasure Hunters
Hardcover 978-0439706308 $19.99
Paperback 978-0439706339 $9.99

#9: Crown of Horns
Hardcover 978-0439706315 $19.99
Paperback 978-0439706322 $9.99
Scholastic/Graphix, 2005-2009
Color, 118-214 pages

BONE COMPANION BOOKS

Bone: Rose
Story by Jeff Smith
Art by Charles Vess

Hardcover 978-0545135429 $18.99
Paperback 978-0545135436 $10.99
Scholastic/Graphix, 2009
Color, 140 pages

Bone: Tall Tales
Stories by Jeff Smith with Tom Sniegoski
Art by Jeff Smith
Colors by Steve Hamaker

Hardcover 978-0545140959 $18.99
Paperback 978-0545140966 $10.99
Scholastic/Graphix, 2010
Color, 118 pages

Bone Handbook
(this is a guide to the Bone series, not a
graphic novel)
Stories by Jeff Smith and Bob Cooper
Art by Jeff Smith, Charles Vess, and Mark Crilley
Colors by Steve Hamaker

Paperback 978-0545211420 $9.99
Scholastic/Graphix, 2010
Color, 128 pages

BONE WHAT'S NEXT ...

The Wizard's Tale
Story by Kurt Busiek
Art by David Wenzel

Hardcover 978-1600105951 $24.99
IDW, 2010
Color, 144 pages

BRAIN CAMP
Story by Susan Kim and Laurence Klavan
Art by Faith Erin Hicks
Colors by Hilary Sycamore

Paperback 978-1596433663 $16.99
First Second, 2010
Color, 160 pages

BRAIN CAMP WHAT'S NEXT ...

Goosebumps series
Story and art by various

Creepy Creatures
Paperback 978-0439841252 $9.99

Terror Trips
Paperback 978-0439857802 $9.99

Scary Summer
Paperback 978-0439857826 $9.99
Scholastic/Graphix, 2006-2007
Black and white, 144 pages each

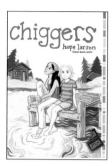

CHIGGERS

Story and art by Hope Larson
Paperback 978-1416935872 $9.99
Simon & Schuster/Aladdin Mix, 2008
Black and white, 176 pages

CHIGGERS WHAT'S NEXT ...

War at Ellsmere

Story and art by Faith Erin Hicks
Paperback 978-1593621407 $12.95
SLG Publishing, 2008
Color, 156 pages

CLAN APIS

Story and art by Jay Hosler, Ph.D.
Paperback 978-0967725505 $20.00
Active Synapse, 2000
Black and white, 160 pages

CLAN APIS WHAT'S NEXT ...

Leo Geo and His Miraculous Journey through the Center of the Earth

Story and art by Jon Chad

Hardcover 978-1596436619 $15.99
Roaring Brook Press, 2012
Black and white, 40 pages

COURTNEY CRUMRIN SERIES

Story and art by Ted Naifeh
Color by Warren Wucinich

Courtney Crumrin and the Night Things
Hardcover 978-1934964774 $19.99

Courtney Crumrin and the Coven of Mystics
Hardcover 978-1934964804 $19.99

Courtney Crumrin and the Twilight Kingdom
Hardcover 978-1934964866 $19.99

Courtney Crumrin's Monstrous Holiday
Hardcover 978-1934964927 $19.99
Oni Press, 2012 (reissue)
Color, 128-144 pages

Also available:

Courtney Crumrin Tales
Story and art by Ted Naifeh

A Portrait of the Warlock as a Young Man
Paperback 978-1932664324 out of print

The League of Ordinary Gentlemen
Paperback 978-1934964682 $5.99
Oni Press, 2005-2011
Black and white, 56 pages each

COURTNEY CRUMRIN WHAT'S NEXT ...

Gunnerkrigg Court series
Story and art by Thomas Siddell

Volume 1: Orientation
Hardcover 978-1932386349 $26.95

Volume 2: Research
Hardcover 978-1932386776 $26.95

Volume 3: Reason
Hardcover 978-1936393237 $26.95
Archaia Studios Press, 2008-2011
Color, 280-296 pages

CROGAN'S ADVENTURES SERIES
Story and art by Chris Schweizer

Crogan's Vengeance
Hardcover 978-1934964064 $14.95

Crogan's March
Hardcover 978-1934964248 $14.95

Crogan's Loyalty
Hardcover 978-1934964408 $14.99
Oni Press, 2008-2012
Black and white, 176-212 pages

CROGAN'S ADVENTURES WHAT'S NEXT ...

Destiny's Hand: Ultimate Pirate Collection
Story by Nunzio DeFilippis and Christina Weir
Art by Melvin Calingo
Paperback 978-1934876732 $14.99
Seven Seas, 2009
Black and white, 496 pages

CROSS GAME SERIES
Story and art by Mitsuru Adachi
Translation by Ralph Yamada (Volume 1) and
Lillian Olsen (Volumes 1-8)

Volume 1
Paperback 978-1421537580 $19.99
Volume 2
Paperback 978-1421537665 $14.99
Volume 3
Paperback 978-1421537672 $14.99
Volume 4
Paperback 978-1421537689 $14.99
Volume 5
Paperback 978-1421537696 $14.99
Volume 6
Paperback 978-1421537702 $14.99
Volume 7
Paperback 978-1421537719 $14.99
Volume 8
Paperback 978-1421537726 $14.99
Viz, 2010-2012
Black and white, 376-576 pages

CROSS GAME WHAT'S NEXT ...

Prince of Tennis series
Story and art by Takeshi Konomi
Translation by Joe Yamazaki

Volume 1
Paperback 978-1591164357 $7.95
Volume 2
Paperback 978-1591164364 $7.95
Volume 3
Paperback 978-1591164371 $7.95
Volume 4
Paperback 978-1591164388 $7.95
Volume 5
Paperback 978-1591164395 $7.95
Volume 6
Paperback 978-1591164401 $7.95
Volume 7
Paperback 978-1591167877 $7.95
Volume 8
Paperback 978-1591168539 $7.95
Volume 9
Paperback 978-1591169956 $7.95
Volume 10
Paperback 978-1421500706 $7.95
Volume 11
Paperback 978-1421502014 $7.95
Volume 12
Paperback 978-1421503370 $7.95
Volume 13
Paperback 978-1421506661 $7.95

Volume 14
Paperback 978-1421506678 $7.95
Volume 15
Paperback 978-1421506685 $7.95
Volume 16
Paperback 978-1421506692 $7.95
Volume 17
Paperback 978-1421506708 $7.95
Volume 18
Paperback 978-1421510941 $7.95
Volume 19
Paperback 978-1421510958 $7.95
Volume 20
Paperback 978-1421510965 $7.95
Volume 21
Paperback 978-1421510972 $7.95
Volume 22
Paperback 978-1421510989 $7.95
Volume 23
Paperback 978-1421514734 $7.95
Volume 24
Paperback 978-1421516462 $7.95
Volume 25
Paperback 978-1421516479 $7.95
Volume 26
Paperback 978-1421516486 $7.95
Volume 27
Paperback 978-1421516493 $7.95
Volume 28
Paperback 978-1421516509 $7.95
Volume 29
Paperback 978-1421516516 $7.95
Volume 30
Paperback 978-1421524313 $7.95
Volume 31
Paperback 978-1421524320 $7.95
Volume 32
Paperback 978-1421524337 $7.95
Volume 33
Paperback 978-1421524344 $7.95
Volume 34
Paperback 978-1421524351 $9.99
Volume 35
Paperback 978-1421528472 $9.99
Volume 36
Paperback 978-1421528489 $9.99
Volume 37
Paperback 978-1421528496 $9.99

Volume 38
Paperback 978-1421528502 $9.99
Volume 39
Paperback 978-1421528519 $9.99
Volume 40
Paperback 978-1421528526 $9.99
Volume 41
Paperback 978-1421528533 $9.99
Volume 42
Paperback 978-1421528540 $9.99
Viz, 2004-2011
Black and white, 176-208 pages

HEREVILLE: HOW MIRKA GOT HER SWORD
Story and art by Barry Deutsch
Hardcover 978-0810984226 $15.95
Abrams/Amulet, 2010
Color, 144 pages

HEREVILLE: HOW MIRKA GOT HER SWORD WHAT'S NEXT ...
Foiled
Story by Jane Yolen
Art by Mike Cavallaro
Paperback 978-1596432796 $15.99
First Second, 2010
Color, 160 pages

HIKARU NO GO SERIES

Story by Yumi Hotta
Art by Takeshi Obata
Supervised by Yukari Umezawa
Translation by Andy Nakatani (volumes 1-12);
Naoko Amemiya (volumes 13-23)
English script supervised by Janice Kim

Volume 1
Paperback 978-1591162223 $7.95
Volume 2
Paperback 978-1591164968 $7.95
Volume 3
Paperback 978-1591166870 $7.95
Volume 4
Paperback 978-1591166887 $7.95
Volume 5
Paperback 978-1591166894 $7.95
Volume 6
Paperback 978-1421502755 $7.95
Volume 7
Paperback 978-1421506418 $7.95
Volume 8
Paperback 978-1421506425 $7.95
Volume 9
Paperback 978-1421510668 $7.95
Volume 10
Paperback 978-1421510675 $7.95
Volume 11
Paperback 978-1421510682 $7.95
Volume 12
Paperback 978-1421515083 $7.95
Volume 13
Paperback 978-1421515090 $7.95
Volume 14
Paperback 978-1421515106 $7.95
Volume 15
Paperback 978-1421521923 $7.95

Volume 16
Paperback 978-1421525846 $7.95
Volume 17
Paperback 978-1421525853 $9.99
Volume 18
Paperback 978-1421528236 $9.99
Volume 19
Paperback 978-1421528243 $9.99
Volume 20
Paperback 978-1421528250 $9.99
Volume 21
Paperback 978-1421528267 $9.99
Volume 22
Paperback 978-1421528274 $9.99
Volume 23
Paperback 978-1421528281 $9.99
Viz, 2004-2011
Black and white, 192-216 pages

HIKARU NO GO WHAT'S NEXT ...

BakéGyamon series
Story and art by Mitsuhisa Tamura
Original concept by Kazuhiro Fujita
Translation by Labaaman, HC Language
Solutions, Inc.

Volume 1
Paperback 978-1421517933 $7.99
Volume 2
Paperback 978-1421517940 $7.99
Volume 3
Paperback 978-1421517957 $7.99
Volume 4
Paperback 978-1421518824 $7.99
Volume 5
Paperback 978-1421521718 $7.99
Viz, 2009
Black and white, 200-216 pages

KID BEOWULF SERIES

Story and art by Alexis E. Fajardo

Kid Beowulf and the Blood-Bound Oath
Paperback 978-0980141917 $15.95

Kid Beowulf and the Song of Roland
Paperback 978-0980141924 $17.95
Bowler Hat Comics, 2008-2010
Black and white, 192-244 pages

KID BEOWULF WHAT'S NEXT ...

Beowulf
Story by Stephan Petrucha
Art by Kody Chamberlain
Paperback 978-0061343902 out of print
HarperCollins, 2007
Color, 96 pages

Usagi Yojimbo series
Story and art by Stan Sakai

Book 1: The Ronin
Paperback 978-0930193355 $15.95

Book 2: Samurai
Paperback 978-0930193881 $15.95

Book 3: The Wanderer's Road
Paperback 978-1560970095 $15.95

Book 4: The Dragon Bellow Conspiracy
Paperback 978-1560970637 $16.95

Book 5: Lone Goat and Kid
Paperback 978-1560970880 $16.95

Book 6: Circles
Paperback 978-1560971467 $16.95

Book 7: Gen's Story
Paperback 978-1560973041 $16.95

Book 8: Shades of Death
Paperback 978-1595822789 $15.99

Book 9: Daisho
Paperback 978-1595822796 $15.99

Book 10: The Brink of Life and Death
Paperback 978-1595822802 $15.99

Book 11: Seasons
Paperback 978-1569713754 $14.99

Book 12: Grasscutter
Paperback 978-1569714133 $16.95

Book 13: Grey Shadows
Paperback 978-1569714591 $14.95

Book 14: Demon Mask
Paperback 978-1569715239 $15.95

Book 15: Grasscutter II: Journey to Atsuta Shrine
Paperback 978-1569716601 $15.95

Book 16: The Shrouded Moon
Paperback 978-1569718834 $15.95

Book 17: Duel at Kitanoji
Paperback 978-1569719732 $16.95

Book 18: Travels with Jotaro
Paperback 978-1593072209 $15.99

Book 19: Fathers and Sons
Paperback 978-1593073190 $15.99

Book 20: Glimpses of Death
Paperback 978-1593075491 $15.99

Book 21: The Mother of Mountains
Paperback 978-1593077839 $15.99

Book 22: Tomoe's Story
Paperback 978-1593079475 $15.99

Book 23: Bridge of Tears
Paperback 978-1595822987 $17.99

Book 24: Return of the Black Soul
Paperback 978-1595824721 $16.99

Book 25: Fox Hunt
Paperback 978-1595827265 $16.99

Usagi Yojimbo: Yokai
Hardcover 978-1595823625 $14.99
Fantagraphics (books 1-7), Dark Horse (books 8+), 1987-2011
Black and white, 64-244 pages

LILA AND ECCO'S DO IT YOURSELF COMICS CLUB

Story and art by Willow Dawson
Hardcover 978-1554534388 $16.95
Paperback 978-1554534395 $7.95
Kids Can Press, 2010
Black and white, 112 pages

LILA AND ECCO'S DO IT YOURSELF COMICS CLUB WHAT'S NEXT ...

Making Comics
Story and art by Scott McCloud
Paperback 978-0060780944 $22.99
HarperCollins, 2006
Black and white, 272 pages

MOUSE GUARD SERIES

Story and art by David Petersen

Fall 1152
Hardcover 978-1932386578 $24.95
Paperback 978-0345496867 $18.95
Winter 1152
Hardcover 978-1932386745 $24.95
Paperback 978-0345496867 $18.95
Archaia Studios Press, 2007-2009
Color, 200 pages each
Legends of the Guard, Vol. 1
Stories and art by Jeremy Bastian, Ted Naifeh, Alex Sheikman, Sean Rubin, Alex Kain, Terry Moore, Lowell Francis, Katie Cook, Guy Davis, Nate Pride, Jason Shawn Alexander, Craig Rousseau, Karl Kerschl, Mark Smylie, João Lemos, and David Petersen
Hardcover 978-1932386943 $19.95
Archaia Studios Press, 2010
Color, 144 pages

MOUSE GUARD WHAT'S NEXT ...

The Hobbit: An Illustrated Edition of the Fantasy Classic
Story by J.R.R. Tolkien
Adapted by Charles Dixon with Sean Deming
Art by David Wenzel
Paperback 978-0345445605 $17.95
Del Rey, 2001
Color, 144 pages

MY BOYFRIEND IS A MONSTER SERIES

#1: I Love Him to Pieces
Story by Evonne Tsang
Art by Janina Görrissen
Paperback 978-0761370796 $9.95
#2: Made for Each Other
Story by Paul D. Storrie
Art by Eldon Cowgur
Paperback 978-0761370772 $9.95
#3: My Boyfriend Bites
Story by Dan Jolley
Art by Alitha E. Martinez
Paperback 978-0761370789 $9.95
#4: Under His Spell
Story by Marie P. Croall
Art by Hyeondo Park
Paperback 978-0761370765 $9.95
#5: I Date Dead People
Story by Ann Kerns
Art by Janina Görrissen
Paperback 978-0761385493 $9.95
Lerner/Graphic Universe, 2010-2012
Black and white (Vols. 1-3, 5), black and white with color (Vol. 4), 128 pages each

MY BOYFRIEND IS A MONSTER WHAT'S NEXT ...

Miki Falls series
Story and art by Mark Crilley

Book One: Spring
Paperback 978-0060846169 $7.99
Book Two: Summer
Paperback 978-0060846176 $7.99
Book Three: Autumn
Paperback 978-0060846183 $7.99

Book Four: Winter
Paperback 978-0060846190 $7.99
HarperCollins, 2007-2008
Black and white, 176 pages each

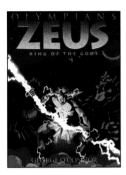

OLYMPIANS **SERIES**
Story and art by George O'Connor

Zeus: King of the Gods
Paperback 978-1596436251 $9.99
Athena: Grey-Eyed Goddess
Paperback 978-0545175326 $9.99
Hera: The Goddess and Her Glory
Paperback 978-0545175326 $9.99
Hades: The Wealthy One
Paperback 978-0545175326 $9.99
First Second, 2009-2012
Color, 80 pages each

OLYMPIANS **WHAT'S NEXT ...**
Percy Jackson and the Olympians: The Lightning Thief: The Graphic Novel
Story by Rick Riordan and Robert Venditti
Art by Attila Futaki
Hardcover 978-1423116967 $19.99
Paperback 978-1423117100 $9.99
Hyperion, 2010
Color, 128 pages

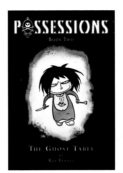

POSSESSIONS **SERIES**
Story and art by Ray Fawkes

Book One: Unclean Getaway
Paperback 978-1934964361 $5.99
Book Two: The Ghost Table
Paperback 978-1934964613 $5.99
Book Three: The Better House Trap
Paperback 978-1934964767 $5.99
Oni Press, 2010-2012
Black and white with green (book 1)
Black and white with blue (book 2)
Black and white with pink (book 3)
80 pages each

POSSESSIONS **WHAT'S NEXT ...**
The Mighty Skullboy Army **series**
Story and art by Jacob Chabot
Volume 1
Paperback 978-1593076290 $9.95
Volume 2
Paperback 978-1595828729 $14.95
Dark Horse, 2007; 2012
Black and white, 88-128 pages

POWER PACK CLASSIC VOL. 1

Story by Louise Simonson
Art by June Brigman, Bob Wiacek, and others
Paperback 978-078513790 $29.99
Marvel, 2009
Color, 256 pages

POWER PACK CLASSIC VOL. 1 WHAT'S NEXT ...

Takio
Story by Brian Michael Bendis
Art by Michael Avon Oeming
Hardcover 978-0785153269 $9.95
Marvel/Icon, 2011
Color, 96 pages

RESISTANCE SERIES

Story by Carla Jablonski
Art by Leland Purvis
Colors by Hilary Sycamore

Book 1: Resistance
Paperback 978-1596432918 $16.99

Book 2: Defiance
Paperback 978-1596432925 $16.99

Book 3: Victory
Paperback 978-1596432932 $17.99
First Second, 2010-2012
Color, 124 pages each

RESISTANCE WHAT'S NEXT ...

A Family Secret
Story and art by Eric Heuvel
Translation by Lorraine Miller
Paperback 978-0374422653 $9.99

The Search
Story by Eric Heuvel, Ruud van der Rol, and Lies Schippers; translation by Lorraine Miller
Paperback 978-0374464554 $9.99
Farrar, Straus and Giroux Books for Young Readers, 2009
Color, 64 pages each

Anne Frank: The Anne Frank House Authorized Graphic Biography
Story by Sid Jacobson and art by Ernie Colón
Hardcover 978-0809026845 $30.00
Paperback 978-0809026852 $16.95
Farrar, Straus and Giroux/Hill and Wang, 2010
Color, 160 pages

SHAZAM! THE MONSTER SOCIETY OF EVIL

Story and art by Jeff Smith
Colors by Steve Hamaker
Hardcover 978-1401214661 $29.99
Paperback 978-1401209742 $19.99
DC Comics, 2007
Color, 208 pages

SHAZAM! THE MONSTER SOCIETY OF EVIL WHAT'S NEXT ...

Batman: The Brave and the Bold series
Story and art by various

The Brave and the Bold
Paperback 978-1401226503 $12.99

The Fearsome Fang Strikes Again
Paperback 978-1401228965 $12.99

Emerald Knight
Paperback 978-1401231439 $12.99
DC Comics, 2010-2011
Color, 128 pages each

SMILE
Story and art by Raina Telgemeier
Colors by Stephanie Yue

Hardcover 978-0545132053 $21.99
Paperback 978-0545132060 $10.99
Scholastic/Graphix, 2010
Color, 218 pages

SMILE WHAT'S NEXT ...

Page by Paige
Story and art by Laura Lee Gulledge
Hardcover 978-0810997219 $18.95
Paperback 978-0810997226 $9.95
Abrams/Amulet, 2011
Black & White, 192 pages

THE STORM IN THE BARN
Story and art by Matt Phelan
Hardcover 978-0763636180 $24.99
Candlewick, 2009
Color, 208 pages

THE STORM IN THE BARN WHAT'S NEXT ...

Wonderstruck
Story and art by Brian Selznick
Hardcover 978-0545027892 $29.99
Scholastic Press, 2011
Black and white, 640 pages

SUPERMAN: SECRET ORIGIN
Story by Geoff Johns
Art by Gary Frank and Jon Sibal
Colors by Brad Anderson
Hardcover 978-1401226978 $29.99
DC Comics, 2010
Color, 224 pages

SUPERMAN: SECRET ORIGIN WHAT'S NEXT ...

Ultimate Spider-Man Vol. 1: Power and Responsibility
Story by Brian Michael Bendis
Art by Mark Bagley

Paperback 978-0785139409 $22.50
Marvel, 2009
Color, 200 pages

TWIN SPICA SERIES

Story and art by Kou Yaginuma
Translation by Maya Rosewood

Volume 1
Paperback 978-1934287842 $10.95
Volume 2
Paperback 978-1934287866 $10.95
Volume 3
Paperback 978-1934287903 $10.95
Volume 4
Paperback 978-1934287934 $10.95
Volume 5
Paperback 978-1935654025 $10.95
Volume 6
Paperback 978-1935654032 $10.95
Volume 7
Paperback 978-1935654124 $10.95
Volume 8
Paperback 978-1935654131 $10.95
Volume 9
Paperback 978-1935654230 $10.95
Volume 10
Paperback 978-1935654247 $10.95
Volume 11
Paperback 978-1935654339 $10.95
Volume 12
Paperback 978-1935654346 $10.95
Vertical, 2010-2012
Black and white, 192-288 pages

TWIN SPICA WHAT'S NEXT ...

Saturn Apartments series
Story and art by Hisae Iwaoka
Translation by Matt Thorn
Volume 1
Paperback 978-1421533643 $12.99
Volume 2
Paperback 978-1421533735 $12.99
Volume 3
Paperback 978-1421533742 $12.99
Volume 4
Paperback 978-1421533759 $12.99
Volume 5
Paperback 978-1421541297 $12.99
Viz, 2010-2012
Black and white, 192 pages each

ULTRA MANIAC SERIES

Story and art by Wataru Yoshizumi
Translation by Koji Goto

Volume One
Paperback 978-1591169178 $8.99
Volume Two
Paperback 978-1591169741 $8.99
Volume Three
Paperback 978-1421500560 $8.99
Volume Four
Paperback 978-1421502045 $8.99
Volume Five
Paperback 978-1421503301 $8.99
Viz, 2005-2006
Black and white, 184 pages each

ULTRA MANIAC SERIES
WHAT'S NEXT ...

Sailor Moon series

Story and art by Naoko Takeuchi

Volume 1
Paperback 978-1935429746 $10.99
Volume 2
Paperback 978-1935429753 $10.99
Volume 3
Paperback 978-1935429760 $10.99
Volume 4
Paperback 978-1612620008 $10.99
Kodansha, 2011-2012
Black and white, 208-244 pages

Cardcaptor Sakura series

Story and art by Clamp
Translation by Mika Onishi and Anita Sengupta

Omnibus Book 1
Paperback 978-1595825223 $19.99
Omnibus Book 2
Paperback 978-1595825919 $19.99
Omnibus Book 3
Paperback 978-1595828088 $19.99
Dark Horse, 2010-2012
Black and white, 576-600 pages

THE UNSINKABLE WALKER BEAN

Story and art by Aaron Renier

Paperback 978-1596434530 $13.99
First Second, 2010
Color, 208 pages

THE UNSINKABLE WALKER BEAN
WHAT'S NEXT ...

Polly and the Pirates

Story and art by Ted Naifeh

Paperback 978-1932664461 $11.95
Oni Press, 2006
Black and white, 176 pages

New Brighton Archeological Society

Story by Mark Andrew Smith
Art by Matthew Weldon

Hardcover 978-1582409733 $17.99
Image, 2009
Color, 179 pages

For Parents, Teachers, and Librarians

A number of resources are available for parents, teachers, and librarians who want to learn more about graphic novels for children and teenagers. The following resources are written by librarians and teachers and will help adults expand their knowledge of graphic novels, find the best graphic novels out there, add graphic novels to their library, and use graphic novels in the classroom.

BOOK RESOURCES

Brenner, Robin. *Understanding Manga and Anime*. Libraries Unlimited, 2007. 356 pages. Hardcover 978-1591583325. $40.

Cornog, Martha and Timothy Perper, eds. *Graphic Novels beyond the Basics: Insights and Issues for Libraries*. Libraries Unlimited, 2009. 281 pages. Paperback 978-1591584780. $45.

Eisner, Will. *Comics and Sequential Art: Principles and Practices from the Legendary Cartoonist*. W.W. Norton & Company, 2008. 192 pages. Paperback 978-0393331264. $22.95.

Goldsmith, Francisca. *The Reader's Advisory Guide to Graphic Novels*. American Library Association, 2009. 136 pages. Paperback 978-0838910085. $45.

Karp, Jesse. *Graphic Novels in Your School Library*. Illustrated by Russ Kress. American Library Association, 2011. 160 pages. Paperback 978-0838910894. $50.

McCloud, Scott. *Making Comics: Storytelling Secrets of Comics, Manga and Graphic Novels*. William Morrow, 2006. 272 pages. Paperback 978-0060780944. $22.99.

McCloud, Scott. *Understanding Comics*. William Morrow, 1994. 224 pages. Paperback 978-0060976255. $22.99.

Monnin, Dr. Katie. *Teaching Early Reader Comics and Graphic Novels*. Maupin House, 2011. 128 pages. Paperback 978-1936700233. $23.95.

Monnin, Dr. Katie. *Teaching Graphic Novels: Practical Strategies for the Secondary ELA Classroom*. Maupin House, 2009. 256 pages. Paperback 978-1934338407. $24.95.

Weiner, Robert G., ed. *Graphic Novels and Comics in Libraries and Archives: Essays on Readers, Research, History and Cataloging*. McFarland, 2010. 288 pages. Paperback 978-0786443024. $45.

BOOKLISTS

Association for Library Service to Children's Graphic Novels Core Collection: *http://www.ala.org/ala/mgrps/divs/alsc/compubs/booklists/grphcnvls.cfm*

Association for Library Service to Children's Notable Children's Books List: *http://www.ala.org/ala/mgrps/divs/alsc/awardsgrants/notalists/ncb/index.cfm* (While this list is not entirely graphic novels, comics are often included.)

Young Adult Library Services Association's Great Graphic Novels for Teens: *http://www.ala.org/yalsa/ggnt* (This list covers graphic novels for teens ages 12-18, so some titles will have more mature content than others.)

WEBSITES FOR REVIEWS AND INFORMATION

Comics Worth Reading: *http://comicsworthreading.com/*

Good Comics for Kids: *http://blog.schoollibraryjournal.com/goodcomicsforkids*

(Full disclosure: Both authors of this book review for GCFK.)

Diamond Bookshelf: *http://bookshelf. diamondcomics.com/public/*

Manga Worth Reading: *http:// comicsworthreading.com/manga-worth-reading/*

No Flying No Tights: *http:// noflyingnotights.com/* (Full disclosure: Snow Wildsmith reviews for and is the review editor at NFNT.)

Publishers Weekly's Graphic Novel News: *http://www.publishersweekly.com/pw/by-topic/book-news/comics/index.html*

Sequential Tart: *http://www. sequentialtart.com/*

Just as is the case with prose fiction and nonfiction, graphic novels are written for all ages, both genders, and a wide variety of interests. Parents who see their kids enjoying graphic novels may want to try to find some that they, as adults and as parents, will enjoy. The best approach is to browse the shelves at local libraries, bookstores, and comics shops. Pick a graphic novel that sounds interesting to *you* and continue the project until you find one that you enjoy.

Some graphic novels speak to the parental experience, and these may be a parent's easiest entry into the format. Here are a few possibilities:

BABY BLUES SERIES

Story and art by Robert Kirkman and Jeremy Scott

Baby Blues: This Is Going to Be Tougher than We Thought
Paperback 978-0809239962 $15.95

She Started It!: Baby Blues Scrapbook #2
Paperback 978-0809232666 out of print

Guess Who Didn't Take a Nap?: Baby Blues Scrapbook #3
Paperback 978-0836217155 out of print

I Thought Labor Ended When the Baby Was Born: Baby Blues Scrapbook #4
Paperback 978-0836217445 out of print

We Are Experiencing Parental Difficulties... Please Stand By: Baby Blues Scrapbook #5
Paperback 978-0836217810 out of print

Night of the Living Dad: Baby Blues Scrapbook #6
Paperback 978-0836213102 $10.95

I Saw Elvis in My Ultrasound: Baby Blues Scrapbook #7
Paperback 978-0836221305 out of print

One More and We're Outnumbered!: Baby Blues Scrapbook #8
Paperback 978-0836226928 out of print

Check, Please...: Baby Blues Scrapbook #9
Paperback 978-0836254235 out of print

Threats, Bribes & Videotape: Baby Blues Scrapbook #10
Paperback 978-0836267501 out of print

If I'm a Stay-at-Home Mom, Why Am I Always in the Car?: Baby Blues Scrapbook #11
Paperback 978-0836278453 out of print

Lift and Separate: Baby Blues Scrapbook #12
Paperback 978-0740704550 $10.95

I Shouldn't Have to Scream More Than Once!: Baby Blues Scrapbook #13
Paperback 978-0740705571 out of print

Motherhood Is Not for Wimps: Baby Blues Scrapbook #14
Paperback 978-0740713934 out of print

Unplugged: Baby Blues Scrapbook #15
Paperback 978-0740723230 out of print

Dad to the Bone: Baby Blues Scrapbook #16
Paperback 978-0740726705 out of print

Never a Dry Moment: Baby Blues Scrapbook #17
Paperback 978-0740733048 $10.95

Two Plus One Is Enough: Baby Blues Scrapbook #18
Paperback 978-0740741401 $10.95

Playdate: Category 5: Baby Blues Scrapbook #19
Paperback 978-0740746659 out of print

Our Server Is Down!: Baby Blues Scrapbook #20
Paperback 978-0740754456 out of print

Something Chocolate This Way Comes: Baby Blues Scrapbook #21
Paperback 978-0740756863 $12.99

Briefcase of Baby Blues: Baby Blues Scrapbook #22
Paperback 978-0740763557 $12.99

Night Shift: Baby Blues Scrapbook #23
Paperback 978-0740768422 $12.99

My Space: Baby Blues Scrapbook #24
Paperback 978-0740780899 $12.99

The Natural Disorder of Things: Baby Blues Scrapbook #25
Paperback 978-0740785405 $12.99

Ambushed! In the Family Room: Baby Blues Scrapbook #26
Paperback 978-0740797408 $12.99

Cut! Baby Blues Scrapbook #27
Paperback 978-1449401825 $12.99

Eat, Cry, Poop: Baby Blues Scrapbook #28
Paperback 978-1449414580 $12.99

Scribbles at an Exhibition: Baby Blues Scrapbook #29
Paperback 978-1449409722
Andrews McMeel, 1991-2011
Black and white with color, 128 pages each

New parents and experienced parents alike will identify with Wanda and Darryl MacPherson and their struggles with parenting three small children. This is a comic-strip collection, not a traditional graphic novel, and as such might be easier for readers uncertain about diving into the comic-book medium.

BUNNY DROP SERIES
Story and art by Yumi Unita

Volume 1
Paperback 978-0759531222 $12.99

Volume 2
Paperback 978-0759531192 $12.99

Volume 3
Paperback 978-0759531208 $12.99

Volume 4
Paperback 978-0759531215 $12.99

Volume 5
Paperback 978-0316210331 $12.99
Yen Press, 2010-2012
Black and white, 208-224 pages

Daikichi gets a shock when he goes to his grandfather's funeral and discovers that the old man had a secret love child. But, when no one else in the family is willing to take the little girl

in, Daikichi suddenly goes from being a bachelor to life as a father. Parents will understand Daikichi's fear of failing his young charge and smile at his earnest desire to be a good father, no matter how much he has to change his life.

CHI'S SWEET HOME SERIES
(see full entry on page 91)

Kids may love watching Chi, the adorable kitten, grow up, but adults will identify with the parents of the family who takes Chi in, as they deal with an apartment that doesn't take pets, housetraining a kitten, and living with an active toddler and a pet.

THE SHINIEST JEWEL: A FAMILY LOVE STORY
Story and art by Marian Henley
Hardcover 978-0446199315 out of print
Springboard Press, 2008
Black and white, 176 pages

Nearing her 50th birthday, Marian decided to adopt a child. This is the humorous, but moving, story of her struggles to adopt, while also dealing with her father's impending death.

THREE SHADOWS
Story and art by Cyril Pedrosa
Paperback 978-1596432390 $16.95
First Second, 2008
Black and white, 272 pages

A father and mother vow to save their son from the shadows that stalk him but, no matter how far they run, they cannot escape the fate that awaits them. This allegorical graphic novel is about the pain of losing a child and the process of grief. Pedrosa's loose art is perfectly suited to this deeply affecting tale.

WITH THE LIGHT: RAISING AN AUTISTIC CHILD SERIES
Story and art by Keiko Tobe

Volume 1
Paperback 978-0759523562 $14.99

Volume 2
Paperback 978-0759523593 $14.99

Volume 3
Paperback 978-0759523845 $14.99

Volume 4
Paperback 978-0759523852 $14.99

Volume 5
Paperback 978-0759524019 $14.99

Volume 6
Paperback 978-0316077330 $14.99

Volume 7
Paperback 978-0316077347 $14.99

Volume 8
Paperback 978-0316194457 $14.99
Yen Press, 2007-2011
Black and white, 528 pages each

When she realizes that something is seriously wrong with her first-born child, Sachiko Azuma must fight to have him correctly diagnosed, then to get him the treatment and education he deserves, while dealing with family disapproval for her son's "bad behavior." Even readers new to reading right-to-left will soon be absorbed in this easy-to-follow (but deeply engaging) story.

YOTSUBA&! SERIES
(see full entry on pages 142-143)

Though kids will laugh at Yotsuba's adventures, the stories will also give parents a reason to smile, as they enjoy Yotsuba's father's laid-back parenting style and the light-hearted antics of his bold child.

ZITS SERIES
Story by Jeremy Scott
Art by Jim Borgman

Zits: Sketchbook #1
Paperback 978-0836268256 $12.99

Growth Spurt: Sketchbook #2
Paperback 978-0836278484 $12.99

Don't Roll Your Eyes at Me, Young Man!: Sketchbook #3
Paperback 978-0740711664 $12.99

Are We an "Us"?: Sketchbook #4
Paperback 978-0740718540 $12.99

Zits Unzipped: Sketchbook #5
Paperback 978-0740723223 $12.99

Busted!: Sketchbook #6
Paperback 978-0740726750 $12.99

Road Trip!: Sketchbook #7
Paperback 978-0740738142 $12.99

Teenage Tales: Sketchbook #8
Paperback 978-0740741449 $12.99

Thrashed: Sketchbook #9
Paperback 978-0740751172 $12.99

Pimp My Lunch: Sketchbook #10
Paperback 978-0740754432 $12.99

Are We out of the Driveway Yet?: Sketchbook #11
Paperback 978-0740761997 $12.99

Rude, Crude, and Tattooed: Sketchbook #12
Paperback 978-0740763571 $12.99

You're Making That Face Again: Zits Sketchbook #13
Paperback 978-0740797347 $12.99

Drive!: Zits Sketchbook #14
Paperback 978-1449401078 $12.99
Andrews McMeel, 1998-2011
Black and white with color, 128 pages each

Both parents who are dreading the coming teen years and those parents whose children have already entered this phase will find something to laugh at in this collection of comic strips about high-school freshman Jeremy Duncan and his long-suffering parents.

HERO WORSHIP!

1000 Comic Books You Must Read is an unforgettable full-color journey through 70 years of heroes, classic characters and grand storytelling. Starting with the introduction of Superman in 1938 and flying through offerings of today, the book by acclaimed comics writer and columnist Tony Isabella is sure to entertain and inform. Arranged by decade, Isabella selects the best of the best, providing color photos of each comic book as well as key information and highlights.

Hard Cover • 8 1/4 x 10 7/8 • 272 pages • 1,000 color photos
By Tony Isabella • Item # Z3599 • $29.99